Examining Poetry

Revised and expanded edition

MICHAEL AND PETER BENTON

Hodder & Stoughton
LONDON SYDNEY AUCKLAND

Also available from the same authors:

Touchstones Volumes 1–5
Poetry Workshop
Double Vision

Cover illustration by kind permission of The Museum of Modern Art, New York: *The Starry Night* (1889) by Vincent Van Gogh, oil on canvas, 29 × 36¹/₄″ (73.7 × 92.1 cm). Collection, The Museum of Modern Art, New York, Acquired through the Lillie P. Bliss Bequest. Photograph © 1990 The Museum of Modern Art, New York.

British Library Cataloguing in Publication Data
Benton, Michael *1939–*
   Examining poetry: a practical guide for 15–18 year olds.
   – Rev. ed.
   1. Poetry in English. Criticism. Techniques
   I. Title   II. Benton, Peter *1942–*
   821′.009

ISBN 0 340 52847 8

First published 1986
Second edition (revised and expanded) 1990
Third impression 1993

Typeset in Palatino by Wearside Tradespools, Fulwell, Sunderland
Printed and bound in Great Britain for the educational division of Hodder and Stoughton Ltd, Mill Road, Dunton Green, Sevenoaks, Kent by Thomson Litho Ltd, East Kilbride

— Contents —

— *Introduction* —

Your poetry lessons in school or college so far will probably have been spent in reading and talking about a variety of poems; you may have 'performed' some aloud, recorded some on tape or made your own anthologies. You will probably have written some of your own poems, too, and may have contributed to wall displays or a duplicated magazine. The purpose of this book is to build on this foundation and to help you develop the skills of talking, reading and writing about poems so that you can both enjoy these activities and approach examination work with confidence.

One important thing to realise is that varied reading, informal chat and creative writing are all ways of enjoying and learning about poetry. Above all, your personal responses to a poem remain vital. This book aims to help you to respond to poetry through close reading and precise writing and to sharpen your critical faculties through the activities it offers. It is not a course, not a solution to the examination problem; but we hope the workbook approach will give you experience in handling poems so that you can cope with the demands of formal written work on your own. The book is designed to help you whether you are working as an individual student or as a member of a class.

Poetry should be a regular and enjoyable part of English work and not be relegated merely to examination fodder. The organisation of our material reflects this principle. Our book is in two parts: *Approaching Poetry* outlines a number of ways in which you can help yourself come to terms with listening to, reading, writing and talking about poems. 'I never know what to say' is often the feeling we have when we are suddenly asked to comment upon a poem we have just read; 'Where do I start?' is a common reaction when we are asked to write an essay. The first three sections of the book set out in broad outline how poems express themselves and how you might best approach them. *How to read a poem* shows how a poem is different from any other form of language. Its meanings cannot be summarised; they are a mixture of sounds, rhythms and associations, as well as personal feelings and ideas, to which you have to be alert. *Listening to the words* stops poetry remaining print-bound and 'lifts the poem off the page' so that you hear and experience its rhythm, pace and tone and begin to develop your own idea of what it means. *Group work on a poem* is a guided way-in to poetry to enable you to read, talk and write positively in a useful sequence of activities. The fourth section, *Making your own notes around a poem*, shows you two ways of recording your thoughts and feelings about poems you have read. Finally, *Talking about a poem* suggests that, after you have made notes about your initial impressions, it is helpful to test your responses against those of others in a small group discussion.

The second part of the book, *Examining Poetry*, is arranged in six teaching sections. The first shows strategies for making and ordering your notes ready for writing them up into essay form. Section 7 has a similar aim where you are asked to deal with two poems at the same time. Section 8 develops this theme by means of paired translations of the same poem. Section 9 looks at some early drafts of two poems to enable you to see how these poems have come into being, and shows how writers and readers carry out complementary activities. The last two sections move closer to course and examination work. Section 10 suggests a wide range of possible approaches to coursework for examination purposes; section 11 focuses primarily on the kinds of strategies that are likely to improve your performance in formal writing under time pressure. To help you with your further study, we have also included a list of poetry books which should be a valuable resource and a glossary of all the technical terms used in this book, along with some others that may be useful.

All the sections give examples of different ways of working with poems. We hope that these will be discussed with your English teacher. Several sections include additional poems for you to work on by yourself. These brief selections need to be augmented from the anthologies the class is using and from other sources indicated in section 12.

Michael and Peter Benton

APPROACHING

POETRY

— 1 How to read —
a poem

1 READING WITH THE EYE

Look at any poem laid out on any page – the very presentation invites us to read it with an eye on the length of the lines, the gaps between sections or verses, the spaces around the words. We read poems differently from the way we read fiction. We see most poems *whole*. Try to look at a poem as you might a painting, a photograph on a record sleeve, or a sculpture, and be aware that the lay-out and associations of the words and your *own* view of them are what really matter.

2 READING WITH THE EAR

Read aloud any poem that appeals to you. Poems invite us to speak them with an ear to the rhythm of the lines, the pace of delivery, the sounds of the words. We listen to poems differently from the way we listen to stories. Try to hear the music of the verse as you speak the words.

3 RESPONDING TO WHAT IS UNIQUE

Each poem is highly individual: it needs to be read at least twice. When you have read a poem through both with eye and with ear try to find its heart. It might be an idea, a feeling, the focal point of a description . . . Jot down some notes to capture the poem's distinctive character.

4 THINKING ABOUT WHAT IS GENERAL

Although each poem is unique, all poems have some features in common. They are:

- made of *words*
- shaped into a particular *form*
- concentrated in their *attention*
- concerned to keep *thinking and feeling* together.

When you are talking or writing about any poem you will find there is something to say about each of these four features.

Let us see how this sequence of activities works out in practice. Colin wrote 'Dissection' some time during the first few weeks of his sixth form course. He was studying A levels in the Arts and, to complement these, he was required to take three periods of 'minority time' Science each week. His first 'practical' turned out to be the dissection of a rat. No doubt he wrote up his scientific account in the approved manner; but he also wrote the piece below. First, read it silently ('with the eye').

— *Dissection* —

This rat looks like it is made of marzipan,
Soft and neatly packaged in its envelope;
I shake it free.
Fingering the damp, yellow fur, I know
That this first touch is far the worst.
    There is a book about it that contains
Everything on a rat, with diagrams
Meticulous, but free from blood
Or all the yellow juices
I will have to pour away.
    Now peg it out:
My pins are twisted and the board is hard
But, using force and fracturing its legs,
I manage though
And crucify my rat.
    From the crutch to the throat the fur is ripped
Not neatly, not as shown in the diagrams,
But raggedly;
My hacking has revealed the body wall
As a sack that is fat with innards to be torn
By the inquisitive eye
And the hand that strips aside.
    Inside this taut, elastic sack is a surprise;
Not the chaos I had thought to find,
No oozing mash; instead of that
A firmly coiled discipline
Of overlapping liver, folded gut;
A neatness that is like a small machine –
And I wonder what it is that has left this rat,
Why a month of probing could not make it go again,
What it is that has disappeared . . .
    The bell has gone; it is time to go for lunch.

I fold the rat, replace it in its bag,
Wash from my hands the sweet
Smell of meat and formalin
And go and eat a meat pie afterwards.
    So, for four weeks or so, I am told,
I shall continue to dissect this rat;
Like a child
Pulling apart a clock he cannot mend.

Colin Rowbotham

Next, read it aloud ('with the ear'). If you are working with one or two others, each of you read out the poem in turn. Read more slowly than the pace of your normal speech. Do not rush this activity; treat it as a performance to be rehearsed and, maybe, discussed.

Now, what is unique about the poem? Without conferring with anyone, spend five minutes or so jotting down your first impressions of 'Dissection'. What details do you notice, for whatever reason? What is the heart (no pun intended) of it? If you are working in a small group, share these impressions with the others.

Finally, what can you say about the four features we mentioned in point 4 on p. 9? Look at your notes again and see if you can add to them. Four questions which may help are:

- What words, phrases or lines stood out as you read the poem?
- How does the poem develop?
- What has caught Colin's attention, both about the rat and about his own reactions?
- What thoughts and feelings does Colin have during the dissection?

Again, these questions are best tackled first by yourself but try to compare notes with your classmates afterwards.

Some of our jottings in response to these questions are as follows:

Words

The words are direct and uncompromising, not only in action sequences ('Now peg it out . . .') but also in the continual use of active verbs ('hacking', 'strips'). This even extends to the more reflective parts of the poem ('probing', 'wash', 'pulling apart'). The words are alive with meanings from:
Sounds e.g. the flat 'a' and hard 't's and 'c's of 'taut, elastic sack' help

to prepare us for the rat as a 'small machine'; 'oozing' sounds thick and glutinous to go with 'mash'.

Rhythm – informal movement of speech, but occasional lines have particular rhythmic characters, e.g.

'My pins are twisted and the board is hard' – heavy stresses to suggest physical effort;

'A firmly coiled discipline/Of overlapping liver, folded gut;' – two compact, tightly organised lines to suggest the 'small machine';

'And I wonder . . . disappeared . . .' – three longer lines, loosely connected, to suggest the writer's wondering.

Associations – some words hint at other contexts ('elastic sack', 'oozing mash'); others jump from the page with their associations ('marzipan' and 'crucify').

Form

A monologue; a thoughtful, single voice is speaking. The tone is sympathetic and inviting. The form is not controlled by conventional rhymes and metres yet there's a strong sense of Colin shaping the experience into a narrative. Each detail falls into place as the dissection proceeds; the poem, like the rat, has 'a firmly coiled discipline'. Both creations have 'a neatness that is like a small machine'.

Attention

I'm a double eavesdropper – looking over Colin's shoulder as he works at the laboratory bench and listening to his thoughts and feelings.

I'm drawn in to the poem: first I'm made to *look* at objects on the bench – the rat, the package, the fur, the textbook diagrams; then I'm compelled to *see* as I watch the rat pinned out on the board; finally, I'm invited to *perceive* and to share Colin's wonder at 'What it is that has disappeared'.

Thinking/feeling

When it ends 'Like a child/Pulling apart a clock he cannot mend' this sums up Colin's thoughts about the precision and orderliness of the 'small machine', his feelings of surprise and pleasure at the discovery, and his unease about his clumsy, destructive actions.

These are *our* jottings. Some of your notes will be similar, some different. However we respond, this poem holds an ironic warning. In probing so closely into the workings of poems, we too run the risk of pulling apart clocks we cannot mend, of losing our pleasure at first reading. It is a difficult balance to hold. In the end, we believe there is a deeper pleasure in *what* is read when this is accompanied by a deeper understanding of *how* this experience has come about.

— 2 *Listening to the* — *words*

Poems can be read 'in the head' but almost certainly as you read you 'hear' the poem. As we suggested earlier, you read with the ear: *you* decide on what voice or voices are appropriate. Rhythm, pace, sound, tone are blended in each poem. Shared reading aloud of poems may help you hear the poem for the first time. Deciding that a line could be read like *this* (and certainly not like *that*) helps you get inside the poem and may give you a fuller understanding. The four poems in this section are chosen for you to perform and offer voices that are strongly contrasting.

In groups

Choose one poem and decide how you will read it aloud. You may choose to split it into different large sections, or into smaller units of sense or into single lines. You may use several voices together or have single voices reading different parts. To take the poem off the page you'll need to listen to the words, to the movement, the rhythm and the tone.

'Jane' by Kathleen Jamie (p. 16)

There are several ways you could work on this poem inspired by Charlotte Brontë's famous novel, *Jane Eyre*. An outline of the novel appears with the poem and you may find it helpful to read that before tackling the poem itself. One possible approach to the poem would be to share the reading – perhaps like this:

- One voice takes the part of the airport public address system ('*Would Miss Jane Eyre . . .*');
- one voice acts as the observer/narrator ('and he thrust himself . . . pale as chalk');
- one voice takes on the flow of Mr Rochester's thoughts ('A bookstore! . . . air-conditioning');
- back to the observer/narrator again for the central section;
- and, finally, the dialogue between Mr Rochester and the clerk on the information desk is followed by
- the observer/narrator's closing words.

'Fe Tek A Stride' by Clive Webster (p. 17)

Noel Coward's old song *Mad Dogs and Englishmen Go Out In The Midday Sun* is the starting point for Clive Webster's 'Fe Tek A Stride', a poem which uses a Creole voice and a relaxed swinging conversational rhythm to tell its story.

Clive Webster writes:

> Here is a poem to be said – not simply read! It comes to you with a 'Creole' flavour. 'Creole' is a word that can be used to refer to a variety of ways of speaking, all of which combine African, Caribbean and European influences on language. I wrote this poem when there was a lot in the newspapers and on TV about the 'Sus' laws; laws that meant people could be stopped and searched by the police when they hadn't actually committed a crime. Rastafarians seemed to get stopped a great deal – so much so that the hero of this poem feels sure he's found out why it is that only mad dogs and Englishmen go out in the midday sun! Many of the words in 'Fe Tek A Stride' are written the way they sound but as well as 'Creole' there will be many 'voices' you can use – including your own!

Decide how you are going to read it – either as a single voice or with three or four readers sharing the verses. Rehearse it and then hear the different versions.

'The Telephone Call' by Fleur Adcock (p. 19)

Try it this way: a narrator's voice for 'They asked me . . . I said . . .' etc.; four or five voices coming on the line from Universal Lotteries; a single voice for the bewildered prizewinner.

'Neighbour' by Norman MacCaig (p. 20)

Although this poem could be read by only a single voice, you could try reading it using several voices – perhaps one for each verse. Think about how the voices could build up a portrait of the Neighbour. Try to find the appropriate pace and tone to capture his life-style. Perhaps the flatness of the Neighbour's life should be conveyed by the flatness of the reading? What do *you* think?

— *Jane* —

'Would Miss Jane Eyre please report to Airport Information. Miss Jane Eyre, please.'
– heard over PA at Heathrow

and he thrust himself into the streams
from every continent – a salmon
shouldering, winding,
searching for a face as pale as chalk.
A bookstore! Surely she'd be there,
peering at the print of worlds she recognised?
No. Nor in the transit lounge
with massive Asian families,
nor the Ladies, weeping beneath
the mounting roar of jets and air-conditioning.
He leaps the stairs – she may be taking
a demure, if plastic, cup of tea –
and surveys the concourse. A dark
hooded bird of prey, he sifts, sifts
the dress of all the nations
for a frock in English grey.
Would he catch her tiny voice
in this damned babble?
The information desk – she shakes her head.
'Shall I page again, Sir?'
He gives a brusque 'No. It was an
off-chance, just an off-chance.'
'Is the lady departing or arriving, Sir,
from where?' But he's striding
from the terminal, and minutes later,
his landrover nudges the northbound carriageway.

Kathleen Jamie

Jane Eyre, a novel by C. Brontë, published in 1847.

The heroine, a penniless orphan, has been left to the care of her aunt, Mrs Reed. Harsh and unsympathetic treatment rouses the spirit of the child, and a passionate outbreak leads to her consignment to Lowood Asylum, a charitable institution, where after some miserable years she becomes a teacher. Thence she passes to be a governess at Thornfield Hall to a little girl, the natural daughter of Mr Rochester, a man of grim aspect and sardonic temper. In spite of Jane Eyre's plainness, Rochester is fascinated by her elfish wit and courageous spirit, and falls in love with her, and she with him. Their marriage is prevented at the last moment by the revelation that he has a wife living, a raving lunatic, kept in seclusion at Thornfield Hall. Jane flees from the Hall, and after nearly perishing on the moors is taken in and cared for by the Rev. St John Rivers and his sisters. Under the influence of the strong personality of Rivers, she nearly consents (in spite of her undiminished love for Rochester) to marry him and accompany him to India. She is prevented by a telepathic appeal from Rochester, and sets out for Thornfield Hall, to learn that the place has been burnt down, and that Rochester, in vainly trying to save his wife from the flames, has been blinded and maimed. She finds him in utter dejection, becomes his wife, and restores him to happiness.
    (*The Oxford Companion to English Literature*, ed. Sir Paul Harvey, OUP)

— *Fe Tek a Stride* —

I man feel
Fe tek a stride
In a deh noon-time sun.
Me is not no daag,
Or Englan man;
Ah jus feel
Fe tek a stride
In a deh noon-time sun.

So ah tek dung I tam soh,
Hung dung I locks,
Jus feel fe stride de street
Fe a few blocks.
No worry wid cyar,
Nor bus nor bike;
Ah jus feel fe tek a licah local hike.

Man feel nice now!
Head dance pon I nek,
Arm swing long soh,
Body a ridim mek:
Breeze pon I face,
Tune in a meh head,
Step two, tree, four pave long;
Life catch hol a me,
Dreada dan dread!

Me golang lef,
Me golang right,
Mek a nex lef,
Mek a nex right;
Eve'ting in sight:
Even horizon ah cum farwerd!

But den, Laawd, but den,
Ah hear one big soun,
One deadly dog-in-a-de-night howl,
Soun fix me a groun,
Swell big like cloud
Castin shadow ova me;
Doubt ova me
Till finaleh, wid a screach an a clatter
A whole batter a dem
Clamp me pon a wall;
Body a squeeze like a finger pon a trigger
An me mood a shatter.

Dem a seh, wha me do deh?
Dem deman, wha me wan deh?
An me seh, 'Walkin, jus walkin.'
Hear dem:
Gwaan wid ya talkin, do it a de station;
Don badda shoutin, deh is no doubtin
You mus a plan sum molestation;
Sum wreckin a creation.

Laawd, Oh Laawd,
Is no wanda de onle two fool
Fe tek a stride in a de noon-time sun
Is a mad daag
Or Englan man!

Clive Webster

'Creole' Glossary

Ah	I
badda	bother
cum	come
daag	dog
dan	than
de, deh	the
dem	them, they
deman	demand
den	then
don	don't
dreada dan dread	expression used to convey a feeling of extreme satisfaction
dung	down
fe	for
fe tek	like taking
finaleh	finally
golang	go along
gwaan	go on
hol	hold
I	me, mine
I man, man	I
Laawd	Lord
licah	little
locks	Dreadlocks
meh	me, my
nek	neck
onle	only
ova	over
pon	on
stride	walk
soh	like so
tam	hat or similar head-dress sometimes worn by Rastafarians
tek	take, taking
wanda	wonder
wha	what
wid	with
ya	you, your

The Telephone Call

They asked me 'Are you sitting down?
Right? This is Universal Lotteries',
they said. 'You've won the top prize,
the Ultra-super Global Special.
What would you do with a million pounds?
Or, actually, with more than a million –
not that it makes a lot of difference
once you're a millionaire.' And they laughed.

'Are you OK?' they asked – 'Still there?
Come on, now, tell us, how does it feel?'
I said 'I just . . . I can't believe it!'
They said 'That's what they all say.
What else? Go on, tell us about it.'
I said 'I feel the top of my head
has floated off, out through the window, revolving like a
flying saucer.'

'That's unusual' they said. 'Go on.'
I said 'I'm finding it hard to talk.
My throat's gone dry, my nose is tingling.
I think I'm going to sneeze – or cry.'
'That's right' they said, 'don't be ashamed
of giving way to your emotions.
It isn't every day you hear
you're going to get a million pounds.

Relax, now, have a little cry;
we'll give you a moment . . .' 'Hang on!' I said.
'I haven't bought a lottery ticket
for years and years. And what did you say
the company's called?' They laughed again.
'Not to worry about a ticket.
We're Universal. We operate
a Retrospective Chances Module.

Nearly everyone's bought a ticket
in some lottery or another,
once at least. We buy up the files,
feed the names into our computer,
and see who the lucky person is.'
'Well, that's incredible' I said.
'It's marvellous. I still can't quite . . .
I'll believe it when I see the cheque.'

'Oh,' they said, 'there's no cheque.'
'But the money?' 'We don't deal in money.
Experiences are what we deal in.
You've had a great experience, right?
Exciting? Something you'll remember?
That's your prize. So congratulations
from all of us at Universal.
Have a nice day!' And the line went dead.

Fleur Adcock

— *Neighbour* —

His car sits outside the house.
It never goes anywhere. Is it
a pet?

When he goes for his morning paper
he makes a perfect right-angle
at the corner.

What does he do at home? Sit at attention?
Or does he stay in the lobby
like a hatstand?

Does his wife know she married
a diagram? That she goes to bed
with a faded blueprint?

When I meet him
he greets me with a smile
he must have bought somewhere.

His eyes are two teaspoons
that have been emptied
for the last time.

Norman MacCaig

— 3 Group work on — a poem

You can use the suggestions below as a 'way-in' to a poem of your own choice, working either on your own or as a member of a group. We think you will find a group approach most helpful – certainly so at first.

If you are working in a group you may find it makes for a more lively discussion if two or three of you move from 1 to 2 to 3 (all the suggestions in 2 are mainly to do with how the *language* of the poem works), and for two or three to move from 1 to 3 to 2 (the suggestions in 3 are mainly to do with *feelings*). Language and feelings cannot really be separated in this way, as you will find once you begin to talk.

Remember, these are only suggestions: you can add to them or shorten them. Some of the ideas will not be much use with some poems. Laid out on the page like this it looks rather a lot to take in and seems all too neat and tidy. Do not worry about it. After using the ideas as a starting-point a few times you will find that you do not need to refer to them very often.

1 In groups, if possible, listen to the poem read aloud. On your own and without discussion, jot down any ideas that come to mind immediately after the first reading. Spend no more than 4–5 minutes on this. Don't concern yourselves with 'meaning'; concentrate on anything that the poem may remind you of, any feelings, however unexpected, it suggests; any kind of atmosphere. There may be nothing: it doesn't matter.

2 Read the poem over to yourselves again – aloud if possible so that you hear it. One member of the group could read the poem or you could share the lines or verses between you. As a group, if possible, underline or circle ideas that occur to you when you ask the following questions. Some people find it very helpful to make notes on the text and jottings in the margin: if you can't do this, a sheet of paper alongside the poem will serve. Share your ideas as a group and talk your way through them after a while:

   (i)   Which lines or images did you like or find particularly striking or strange even if you didn't quite understand them?
   (ii) Jot down one or two questions about the poem that you would like answered.

(iii) Look at the poem on the page – at arm's length if you like – what do you notice about its appearance? What is its shape? regular verses? a short single block? sprawling across the page? short lines? long lines? Anything else? The writer decided to present the poem in this way: are there any obvious reasons for his decision?

(iv) Look more closely. Is it written in a form you recognise such as a *haiku, free verse, rhymed verse, syllabic verse, a ballad, a sonnet* . . . ? It's quite possible that you will not recognise a form and it is really not all that important that you should.

(v) Ring round or note anything that seems to form a pattern. It might be a line, a word or an idea that is repeated from time to time. It might be a sound that is repeated or a mental picture that recurs. There may be comparisons (similes or metaphors) that are repeated. Are any such ideas or images linked or developed in any way?

(vi) What do you notice about the language of the poem? Is there a frequent use of adjectives and/or adverbs – if so, do they have any common theme? Is the poem written in the past, present or future tense? Does the tense change at any point?

(vii) How does the poem seem to 'move'? Do the sound and rhythm of the lines seem light and bubbly, for example, or do the lines move slowly with heavy rounded sounds and a slow rhythm? Are the sounds and rhythms different at different places in the poem? Does the punctuation, or lack of it, help you to see how the poem might be read? Do the lines run on into each other without a break, for example, or are their ends sharply marked by punctuation? Try parts of it out by saying them aloud and listening.

3 Read the poem through again and try to think of words that suggest the *mood* of the piece. Does it feel happy, sad, sentimental, defiant, thoughtful, triumphant, unemotional? On your own, jot down the words you think of. Compare yours with those jotted by others in the group. Talk about why you made the choices you did.

(i) Does the poem seem to develop a line of argument? (For example one line might start with the word 'If' and further down there might be a line beginning 'Then', 'So' or 'But' – all words that might advance an argument.) Does it move to a conclusion, a particular point of view at the end? Note any key words in the development of such a line of thought.

(ii) Is it the poet's voice speaking in the poem or is it the voice of somebody else, real or imagined?

(iii) Is the poet speaking out to you? quietly reflecting to himself/herself? addressing the world in general . . . ? If there is another voice in the poem, is it doing the same?

(iv) How does the poet feel about you, the reader? Are you being asked to share something personal? Are you being pleaded with, mocked or laughed at, preached at? Is the poet trying to teach you, persuade you, move you, entertain you . . . something else? How do you know this?

(v) How does the poet feel about the subject of the poem? Are you being offered a message or a view of things that the writer wants you to share or understand? If so, think about why this might be. Does the poem's title suggest anything about the writer's feelings?

4 (i) Look back at your first notes where you jotted down questions you wanted answering. Have you found answers now? If not, can anyone in the group help?

(ii) Read the poem again in the light of your thoughts and notes. Make any further jottings. Relax. Read it again.

— 4 Making your own — notes around a poem

We have already stressed that reading a poem means 'seeing it whole'. When reading and rereading, some parts of a poem may seem clear, others hazy; often we seem to find several different points of entry as we build up the details of the picture. We take a sort of mental walk round the poem. We want to encourage you now to use a note pad on this walk.

Below are two examples of the sort of notes that can be made on first reading a poem. Experiment with both methods of jotting and see which you feel most at ease with. The first invites you to log your feelings and ideas by arranging them around a poem; the second is a way of mapping your responses in close detail.

Logging your thoughts

Read Edward Thomas's 'Cock-Crow' (p. 25) first. Then follow our thought-track around the poem.

Now, make your own notes about one or more of the poems on pp. 25–8. Try to follow the sequence of first thoughts, second thoughts, etc. as we have done. Here, as in the second method (p. 29), it is best to work on a copy of the poem you choose. All the poems are short enough to write out on a single sheet of paper. This task itself will slow down your reading to writing pace and help you to attend closely to the words.

Compare notes with a partner only when you have spent five or ten minutes on your own jottings.

1st thoughts
- being woken up by two cocks crowing together

- last line < let down feeling
           < just getting light

6th thoughts
- carefully worked regular shape:
  2 long lines, alt. with broken line. Useful esp. in 'Heralds . . . hand, Each . . . each' = framed.

5th thoughts
lots of opposites like this:
the world   . . . the real world
inside his head . . . *outside*
thoughts   . . . actions
night   . . . light
growth   . . . cutting down
darkness   . . . silver

2nd thoughts on re-reading
- why 'wood of thoughts'?
- I like the *sounds* – words and rhymes.
- image chain: wood grows/ cut down/axe/cleave/silver blow
- visual impact of heraldic tableau.

3rd thoughts
relation of world in his head and world outside = between visual images and sound of cock-crow.

4th thoughts re last 4 lines
contrast between
static   . . . moving
near, local . . . distanced
stylised   . . . earthy, everyday
colourful . . . colourless
noble   . . . peasant

— Cock-Crow —

Out of the wood of thoughts that grows by night
To be cut down by the sharp axe of light,
Out of the night, two cocks together crow,
Cleaving the darkness with a silver blow:
And bright before my eyes twin trumpeters stand,
Heralds of splendour, one at either hand,
Each facing each as in a coat of arms:
The milkers lace their boots up at the farms.

Edward Thomas

— Cat —

Sometimes I am an unseen
marmalade cat, the friendliest colour,
making off through a window without permission,
pacing along a broken-glass wall to the
    greenhouse,
jumping down with a soft, four-pawed thump,
finding two inches open of the creaking door
with the loose brass handle,
slipping impossibly in,
flattening my fur at the hush and touch of
    the sudden warm air,
avoiding the tiled gutter of slow green water,
skirting the potted nests of tetchy cactuses,
and sitting with my tail flicked
skilfully underneath me, to sniff
the azaleas   the azaleas   the azaleas.

Alan Brownjohn

— *The Butterfly* —

There is no story behind it.
It is split like a second.
It hinges around itself.

It has no future.
It is pinned down to no past.
It's a pun on the present.

It's a little yellow butterfly.
It has taken these wretched hills
under its wings.

Just a pinch of yellow,
it opens before it closes
and closes before it o

where is it

Arun Kolatkur

— *Clown* —

He was safe
behind the whitened face
and red nose of his trade,
vocation more certain
than doctor's or priest's
to cheer and heal.
Hidden away from himself
he could always make us laugh
turning troubles like jackets
inside out, wearing
our rents and patches.
Tripping up in trousers too long
he made us feel tall;
and when we watched him
cutting himself down,
missing the ball,
we knew we could cope.

What we never knew
was the tightrope he walked
when the laughter had died.
Nowhere to hide in the empty night,
no one to catch his fall.

Phoebe Hesketh

— *Shantytown* —

High on the veld upon that plain
And far from streets and lights and cars
And bare of trees, and bare of grass,
Jabavu* sleeps beneath the stars.   * Shantytown area near Johannesburg

Jabavu sleeps.
The children cough.
Cold creeps up, the hard night cold,
The earth is tight within its grasp,
The highveld cold without soft rain,
Dry as the sand, rough as a rasp
The frost rimmed night invades the shacks.
Through dusty ground
Through rocky ground
Through freezing ground the night cold creeps.
In cotton blankets, rags and sacks
Beneath the stars Jabavu sleeps.

One day Jabavu will awake
To greet a new and shining day;
The sound of coughing will become
The children's laughter as they play
In parks with flowers where dust now swirls
In strong-walled homes with warmth and light.
But for tonight Jabavu sleeps.
Jabavu sleeps. The stars are bright.

Anonymous (South Africa)

— *Lady Godiva*[1] —

How little I know of you,
Golden-maned lady!
Not the why of your exile,
Not what happened later . . .
Just a snippet of a legend
Tells your wordless triumph
Over that high and mighty churl,
Tells how shuttered windows
Served you as shield,
And a disciplined popular will:
No mocking allowed!
(How can one help but love the English?)
A town without people,
All its gates shut tight:
Not a soul unless
You count the executioner.
Did this executioner exist?

Maybe I just invented him?
But in such affairs
Can he be avoided?
As a judge will play the devil,
A gravedigger dig the grave,
So the executioner stands waiting
Beside every deathless road.
But the executioner's eyes
Can't be seen through the slit in his hood,
As it was and always has been –
(Perhaps they're not meant to have eyes?)
In the whole world, just those two:
The Earl of Mercia on his balcony,
The eyeless executioner,
See you off into exile.
The drumming of hooves
Dies away along empty streets
Like a forgotten word
Plunged into rustling centuries.

Here time has jammed in still motion,
And the wind doesn't dare to touch
The inconceivable cloak
Of heavy hair.
Oh, courageous lady,
Let's fearlessly spur the horse,
Ride straight ahead,
Not counting centuries or minutes!
Let's slice executions and epochs
Like pieces of layer cake,
And cut through other epochs
Following close on our heels!
We'll wear a hole in history –
When was it sorry for us?
We'll take a corner off the town's town hall,
Frighten the pettifoggers,
Break into somebody else's years
With our crazy steed
Reflecting the divided world
In one astonished pupil!

Small Zone, January 1985[2]

Irina Ratushinskaya (trans. Lyn Coffin with Sergei Shiskoff)

[1] Lady Godiva was the wife of Leofric, Earl of Mercia, one of Edward the Confessor's great earls. According to legend, her husband having imposed a tax on the inhabitants of Coventry, she pleaded with him to remit it, which he jokingly promised to do if she would ride naked through the streets at noon. She took him at his word, directed the people to stay indoors and shut all windows, and complied with his condition. Peeping Tom, who looked out, was struck blind.

[2] Irina Ratushinskaya was imprisoned in March 1983 for writing poetry that was judged to be 'anti-Soviet agitation and propaganda'. She was sentenced to seven years' hard labour. She spent three years in the Small Zone, a special unit for women prisoners of conscience. Many of the poems she wrote there were first written with burnt matchsticks on to bars of soap and then memorised. She was released in October 1986 just before the Reykjavik summit meeting of Mikhail Gorbachev and Ronald Reagan.

Mapping your responses

This approach will help you discover *how* you read a poem and enable you to compare your 'readings' with those of other students.

First, try the following sequence of activities with Robert Frost's poem 'The Lockless Door' shown below. As before, it is best to work on your own copy.

— *The Lockless Door* —

It went many years,
But at last came a knock,
And I thought of the door
With no lock to lock.

I blew out the light,
I tiptoed the floor,
And raised both hands
In prayer to the door.

But the knock came again
My window was wide;
I climbed on the sill
And descended outside.

Back over the sill
I bade a 'Come in'
To whatever the knock
At the door may have been.

So at a knock
I emptied my cage
To hide in the world
And alter with age.

Robert Frost

Individually, carry out the following three steps:

- Read the poem to yourself in the normal way. Note down how many times you read it before making your first jotting.

- Jot down your own responses to the poem, *numbering them in sequence as you go*. Your jottings might be about mental pictures you have during the reading, memories or associations that the poem brings to mind, any puzzling bits, the feelings the words give you at different points and so on.
- Now, on a separate sheet make a simple diagram of your 'reading' by ruling five horizontal lines (one for each of the five verses) and plotting the numbers on to your diagram in the appropriate places. Use solid lines to represent continuous reading and responses, and broken lines to show where you jump from one part of the poem to another. Show by vertical lines how many times you read the poem before your first jotting.

Here is an example from Sara, a GCSE student. She read the poem twice and then made these notes:

— *The Lockless Door* —

It went many years,
But at last came a knock,
And I thought of the door
With no lock to lock.

I blew out the light,
I tiptoed the floor,
And raised both hands
In prayer to the door.

But the knock came again.
My window was wide;
I climbed on the sill
And descended outside.

Back over the sill
I bade a 'Come in'
To whatever the knock
At the door may have been.

So at a knock
I emptied my cage
To hide in the world
And alter with age.

Robert Frost

Sara's handwritten annotations:

1 Image of a flat, dirty and old. A battered door, closed tightly, open window with roof falling away steeply below. No person.

2 Why?

3 eerie feeling

4 The person involved seems to be scared and frightened of the outside world.

5 Another image is of a prison cell. A prisoner being freed but not wanting to face the world after being shut away for so long.

6 Locked in somewhere nowhere to go

7 waiting helplessly for a knock to come

8 the mind?

9 praying for what? The person to go away. Why?

10 maybe frightened of seeing someone

11 importance of last line

12 not a person knocking, something, a memory.

Sara's diagram looked like this:

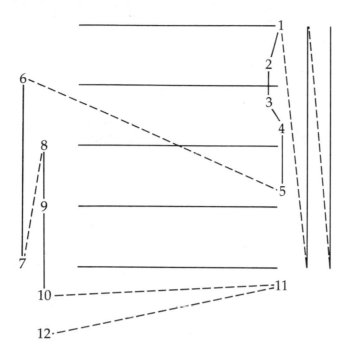

Sara was reading carefully but still finding the poem a puzzle. She commented:

Sara   The Lockless Door

Read it thragh a cuple of times. I noticed that the last line was important. The last verse was very strong and hard to understand. My mind created an image almost at once. A dirty flat with a solid wooden door with paint peeling off it. The window was small and open. The place was bare, shadowy and musty, the window didn't let in much light.

I'm not sure that the image really helped me to understand the poem, as now I don't think the poem has anything to do with people knocking on a door. The poem created an eerie, sensitive feeling, the person involved seemed to be frightened and scared of something, maybe the World. I felt really sorry for him or her.

The picture of a prison cell then come to me, but climbing out of the window contradicts this. I kept reading the poem over and over, but I still can't understand it.

- How does your 'reading' compare with Sara's?
- *In groups*, ask yourselves what your diagrams tell you about how you read the poem. Are there any bits that most of you have commented on? Did you have the same pictures in your mind's eye? Are there any key lines or ideas which sum up the poem for you?
- Try out this sequence of activities with one or more of the following poems. As you become used to jotting down your responses in this way and comparing notes with others in your group (you don't have to do diagrams every time!), your confidence in reading poetry will increase. That's not surprising because close attention like this is the reader's version of what the writer does when making a poem (see section 9). Both poets and their readers use jottings. Choose one of these poems to start with.

— *Hot Summer Sunday* —

Especially on hot summer Sundays
my Grandpa liked to rest
supine in the narrow bathtub
soaking in curved cool water
sometimes flipping his toes
or, quite child-like,
toying with a pale green soapcake,
but mostly
staying motionless, eyes closed,
lips half-smiling,
limbs outstretched.

That hot summer Sunday
when I looked at him
straightly lying, lips parted,
silent in the shallow trough,
a foam of white, frothed and lacy,
set as new suds
about his shaven jawbones,
it seemed he might stir,
whistle a relaxed sigh,
unclose those eyelids,
ask me to scrub his back.

A. L. Hendriks

— *Song for the Old Ones* —

My Fathers sit on benches
   their flesh count every plank
   the slats leave dents of darkness
deep in their withered flanks.

They nod like broken candles
   all waxed and burnt profound,
   they say 'It's understanding
that makes the world go round.'

There in those pleated faces
   I see the auction block
   the chains and slavery's coffles*
the whip and lash and stock.

*a train of slaves
  driven along together

My Fathers speak in voices
   that shred my fact and sound
   they say 'It's our submission
that makes the world go round.'

They used the finest cunning
   their naked wits and wiles
   the lowly Uncle Tomming
and Aunt Jemimas' smiles.

They've laughed to shield their crying
   then shuffled through their dreams
   and stepped 'n fetched a country
to write the blues with screams.

I understand their meaning
   it could and did derive
   from living on the edge of death
They kept my race alive.

Maya Angelou

— *The Prodigal Son* —

I could remember nothing of the village:
Only, at a sharp elbow in the lane
Between the train-station and the first cottage,
An August cornfield flowing down to meet me;
At its dry rim a spatter of scarlet poppies.

I had forgotten the cement-botched church,
The three spoilt bells my grandmother had christened
Crock, Kettle and Pan; the cider-sharp Devon voices,
The War Memorial with my uncle's name
Spelt wrongly, women in working black, black stockings,
White aprons, sober washing lines, my Bramley-
Cheeked aunt picking blackberries in her cap,
The butcher's cart, the baker's cart from Chudleigh,
From Christow, and the hard-lipped granite quarry
Coughing up regular dust under the skyline.

But this came later. I heard as I climbed
The white flint lane the still-insistent voices:
'Never go back,' they said. 'Never go back.'
This was before the fall of corn, the poppies.

Out of the sun's dazzle, somebody spoke my name.

Charles Causley

— *Solo* —

Following the sun
each one turns on his own axis.
You never can get in
to the spin of another –
mother, father, sister, lover
indwelling, encased
as snails that shrink at a finger-tip.

Talk of family, community
and unity of two:
each birth, each death is separate.
We follow our star, hear our bell
toll, yet share
only one common fate –
a heaven-and-hell
that's private, personal, inviolate.

Phoebe Hesketh

— *The Warm and the Cold* —

Freezing dusk is closing
  Like a slow trap of steel
On trees and roads and hills and all
  That can no longer feel.
    But the carp is in its depth
      Like a planet in its heaven,
    And the badger in its bedding
      Like a loaf in the oven.
    And the butterfly in its mummy
      Like a viol in its case.
    And the owl in its feathers
      Like a doll in its lace.

Freezing dusk has tightened
  Like a nut screwed tight
On the starry aeroplane
  Of the soaring night.
    But the trout is in its hole
      Like a chuckle in a sleeper.
    The hare strays down the highway
      Like a root going deeper.
    The snail is dry in the outhouse
      Like a seed in a sunflower.
    The owl is pale on the gatepost
      Like a clock on its tower.

Moonlight freezes the shaggy world
  Like a mammoth of ice –
The past and the future
  Are the jaws of a steel vice.
    But the cod is in the tide-rip
      Like a key in a purse.
    The deer are on the bare-blown hill
      Like smiles on a nurse.
    The flies are behind the plaster
      Like the lost score of a jig.
    Sparrows are in the ivy-clump
      Like money in a pig.

Such a frost
  The flimsy moon
    Has lost her wits.

    A star falls.

The sweating farmers
  Turn in their sleep
    Like oxen on spits.

Ted Hughes

— 5 Talking about a — poem

A group of five students talked about 'The Warm and the Cold' (p. 35). We thought it would be helpful to you in your own groups to eavesdrop on parts of their conversation and to test out your ideas of the poem against theirs.

They had some questions which you may be able to answer; they may have some answers to questions you have raised.

Reading written-down speech is difficult if you are not used to it. Why not cast it and read it as a play?

Extract 1

Graham	'a chuckle in a sleeper.' What's a 'chuckle in a sleeper'?*
Tom	Oh yes.
Nick	Well, a sleeper could be –
Zoe	A railway sleeper –
Graham	A railway sleeper, yeah, so a chuckle might be –
Tom	Yeah – or a sleeper can be a person sleeping.
Graham	Or a train. (*laughter*)
Tom	I mean – erm –
Zoe	What's the chuckle bit then?

---

* *What do you think it means?*

Extract 2

Zoe	'The past and the future/Are the jaws of a steel vice.'
Nick	That's pretty stupid.
Tom	Yeah. Suppose it could mean the two things coming together.
Zoe	It's being held together.
Tom	Yeah, well the two things, the past and the future, coming together into the present –
Nick	Means you can't separate them.* – You can't really, can you?
Zoe	Well they're frozen together.

---

* *Nick begins to see an idea in the line Zoe quotes.*
Can you take it further?

Extract 3

Graham	'Such a frost/The flimsy moon/Has lost her wits' –
Zoe	– and then 'sweating farmers' –
Graham	Yeah, and then he breaks it with 'A star falls'
Zoe	Yes
Graham	'A star falls' –
Tom	I wonder why he did that – break it with 'A star falls'?*
Zoe	Why is there 'A star falls'?

* *Why do you think the structure of the poem changes here?*

Extract 4

Graham	'The deer on the . . .'. What about 'The deer are on the bare-blown hill/Like smiles on a nurse'?
Zoe	I don't get that.
Graham	No, it doesn't seem like all this. The others kind of relate – the cod, and the key in the purse, kind of relate more than 'the deer on . . .'
Tom	Yeah, What is . . . I mean it's got fish in all three here – 'the carp's in its depth/Like a planet in its heaven' then 'the trout's in its hole/Like a chuckle in a sleeper' – erm – and 'the cod's in the tide – rip/Like a key in a purse.' It must all relate somehow.
Graham	The first verse is always fish – . . . Up here you've got the first four lines then you've got fish.*

* *Can you see any other patterns?*

Extract 5

Nick	One thing about this poem is that it's a lot of effort to read it –
Graham	Yeah
Tom	Yeah. Some poems –
Zoe	– On your own. It's not so much effort when you're doing it all together but on your own – to get right into it like we have done –
Graham	But in class –
Tom	– we wouldn't bother really looking.

> Graham — you can't really say what you want to say if you've got a teacher in there, because the teacher's got their own ideas on it, hasn't he?
>
> Tom   Exactly! Exactly! They don't really listen to us a lot.
>
> Lucy   You can't analyse it just by first look – you have to go into it.
>
> Tom   You've got to read it.
>
> Zoe   You've got to go into it.*
>
> Tom   Yeah. They can put forward their ideas – say what they – say what they think about it, you know – but they should, they should let us have a go as well. It's no good just saying – er – 'Do you agree with me?' You're bound to say yes.
>
> Zoe   And you daren't say no.
>
> Tom   And normally you're asked to write a poem . . .

** Do you *have* any ideas about the best way of tackling poems?*

EXAMINING POETRY

— 6 Studying single — poems

In the first part of the book we have concentrated upon reading, listening, talking and note-making as basic activities in approaching poetry. Now we want to help you organise your ideas towards more formal writing by building upon these 'basics'.

With both the examples shown below, carry out the following sequence of activities *before* you move on to our notes.

Reading. Read the poem silently; read it aloud as a member of a small group. Charles Causley's poem can be shared between two voices; 'Metaphors' might be read one line per person around a group.

Note-making. Individually, make your own notes around the poems, as in section 4.

Discussion. In pairs or small groups, talk about the poems and the things you have jotted down.

Drafting. Use your notes to answer these three questions about each poem: 1 What sort of poem is it? 2 How does it work? 3 What do I feel about it?

— Mary, Mary Magdalene —

On the east wall of the church of St Mary Magdalene at Launceston in Cornwall is a granite figure of the saint. The children of the town say that a stone lodged on her back will bring good luck.

Mary, Mary Magdalene
Lying on the wall,
I throw a pebble on your back.
Will it lie or fall?

Send me down for Christmas
Some stockings and some hose,
And send before the winter's end
A brand-new suit of clothes.

Mary, Mary Magdalene
Under a stony tree,
I throw a pebble on your back.
What will you send me?

I'll send you for your christening
A woollen robe to wear,
A shiny cup from which to sup,
And a name to bear.

Mary, Mary Magdalene
Lying cool as snow,
What will you be sending me
When to school I go?

I'll send a pencil and a pen
That write both clean and neat,
And I'll send to the schoolmaster
A tongue that's kind and sweet.

Mary, Mary Magdalene
Lying in the sun,
What will you be sending me
Now I'm twenty-one?

I'll send you down a locket
As silver as your skin,
And I'll send you a lover
To fit a gold key in.

Mary, Mary Magdalene
Underneath the spray,
What will you be sending me
On my wedding-day?

I'll send you down some blossom,
Some ribbons and some lace,
And for the bride a veil to hide
The blushes on her face.

Mary, Mary Magdalene
Whiter than the swan,
Tell me what you'll send me,
Now my good man's dead and gone.

I'll send to you a single bed
On which you must lie,
And pillows bright where tears may light
That fall from your eye.

Mary, Mary Magdalene
Now nine months are done,
What will you be sending me
For my little son?

I'll send you for your baby
A lucky stone, and small,
To throw to Mary Magdalene
Lying on the wall.

Charles Causley

— *Metaphors* —

I'm a riddle in nine syllables,
An elephant, a ponderous house,
A melon strolling on two tendrils.
O red fruit, ivory, fine timbers!
This loaf's big with its yeasty rising.
Money's new-minted in this fat purse.
I'm a means, a stage, a cow in calf.
I've eaten a bag of green apples,
Boarded the train there's no getting off.

Sylvia Plath

— *Mary, Mary Magdalene* —

*On the east wall of the church of St Mary Magdalene at Launceston
in Cornwall is a granite figure of the saint. The children of the town
say that a stone lodged on her back will bring good luck.*

Mary, Mary Magdalene
Lying on the wall,
I throw a pebble on your back.
Will it lie or fall?

Who is speaking? A child's voice, chanting a rhyme. What is happening? Child throws a pebble on to the stone figure of the saint./Local superstition and Christian belief brought together. Sing-song rhythm/nursery rhymes/ games.

Send me down for Christmas
Some stockings and some hose,
And send before the winter's end
A brand-new suit of clothes.

Child makes wishes (pebble must have stayed there). Oddly old-fashioned feel about Christmas wishes for clothes. 'Hose', too, is archaic; and 'stockings' and 'brand new suit' for a *young* child. Edwardian feel.

1st age: the baby
More stone decoration 'stony tree'.
The first question addressed to M.M.

Mary, Mary Magdalene
Under a stony tree,
I throw a pebble on your back.
What will you send me?

*I'll send you for your christening
A woollen robe to wear,
A shiny cup from which to sup,
And a name to bear.*

Who is speaking? M.M. replies: the good luck for the baby is to be named, to be clothed and to be fed – the basics of life.

2nd age: the schoolgirl
Child-like urgency in repeated 1st line address to saint and insistent questions. M.M. 'cool as snow' suggests innocence of childhood; perhaps the white granite, too. The coolness is emphasised by internal rhyme of 'cool' – 'school' as well as the normal end rhymes.

Mary, Mary Magdalene
Lying cool as snow,
What will you be sending me
When to school I go?

*I'll send a pencil and a pen
That write both clean and neat,
And I'll send to the schoolmaster
A tongue that's kind and sweet.*

Maternal care in saint's language: 'clean', 'neat', 'kind', 'sweet'.

Mary, Mary Magdalene
Lying in the sun,
What will you be sending me
Now I'm twenty-one?

I'll send you down a locket
As silver as your skin,
And I'll send you a lover
To fit a gold key in.

Mary, Mary Magdalene
Underneath the spray,
What will you be sending me
On my wedding-day?

I'll send you down some blossom,
Some ribbons and some lace,
And for the bride a veil to hide
The blushes on her face.

Mary, Mary Magdalene
Whiter than the swan,
Tell me what you'll send me,
Now my good man's dead and
    gone.

I'll send to you a single bed
On which you must lie,
And pillows bright where tears may
    light
That fall from your eye.

Mary, Mary Magdalene
Now nine months are done,
What will you be sending me
For my little son?

I'll send you for your baby
A lucky stone, and small,
To throw to Mary Magdalene
Lying on the wall.

Charles Causley

3rd age: the lover
Saint's figure is now seen as warm in the sun; suits the woman anticipating her lover.

Sexual imagery: gold key/silver locket; sensuality of 'skin'.

4th age: the bride
Another bit of stonework: 'spray' part of 'the stony tree'?

Feeling of rich, summery colours: 'blossom', 'ribbons', 'blushes' to celebrate the wedding – balanced by the coyness/reserve of the internal rhyme 'bride' . . . 'hide'.

5th age: the widow
The white/swan link suggests death (contrast snow in vs. 5). Solemn note – '. . . good man's dead and gone' – down-to-earth, matter-of-fact acceptance; old-fashioned, rustic 'feel'.

Loneliness of 'single bed'; sadness of loss of loved one. Curious 'bright'/'light' internal rhyme makes the weeping into the pillow stylised rather than 'felt emotion'. Ritual grieving/mourning suggest inevitability of death; no sentimentality.

6th age: the mother
The cycle starts again. Normally, we'd expect 5th/6th ages in reverse order. This way Causley can complete the cycle with new born baby.

M.M. ends poem both optimistically ('lucky stone'), and yet resigned to inevitability of cycle of life and death.

1 What sort of poem is it?

2 How does it work?

3 What do I feel about it?

1
- It is a story shared between two voices, those of the girl and the saint; a story that ends where it began.
- It plots the 'six ages of woman'. The poem is organised in pairs of verses which, after the introductory pair, alternate the voices of the girl and the Saint in the six subsequent pairs.
- Its language and form are those of a ballad. Descriptions are clear and unqualified by adjectives and adverbs; objects are included simply to stand for one of the 'ages', not for detailed description. The form is like that of a nursery rhyme.

2 My detailed notes above would lead me to expand on these three points – perhaps a paragraph on each:
- *the story of the poem.* The life-cycle marked by its main turning-points/ceremonies. It's circular: by reversing 'widow' and 'mother', Causley can complete one cycle with a new born baby and simultaneously imply the start of another.
- *the shape of the poem.* The first two verses set up the situation of making wishes when the pebble lodges on the stone saint. Then each subsequent pair focuses in turn on the baby, the schoolgirl, the lover, the bride, the widow and the mother. It's as regular and ordered as a ritual.
- *the language of the poem.* An old-fashioned (Edwardian?) feel (vs. 2) seems to distance the poem in time. The girl's description of the saint (first verse of each pair) changes according to the 'age' ('under a stony tree' for the baby vs. 3; 'cool as snow' for the schoolgirl vs. 5; 'lying in the sun' for the lover vs. 7, etc. . . .). Mary Magdalene's reply is characterised by appropriate objects (name, clothes, food for baby vs. 4; pencil and pen for schoolgirl vs. 6; sexual imagery of key and locket for lover vs. 8, etc. . . .) which are emblems for that 'age'.

3 Overall, it's a poem I like for its order and completeness. It's not personal; the poet doesn't tell me directly about his feelings. But I do get a sense of his ambivalent feelings at the end about the cycle of life he has described. For the poem ends optimistically with the 'lucky stone' and the idea of growth and continuity; yet there's the sense of resigned inevitability at the cycle of life and death in the last verse. Increasingly, too, the bright, lively tone of the nursery rhyme rhythms are offset by the growing sense that human life falls into a pattern we have to accept.

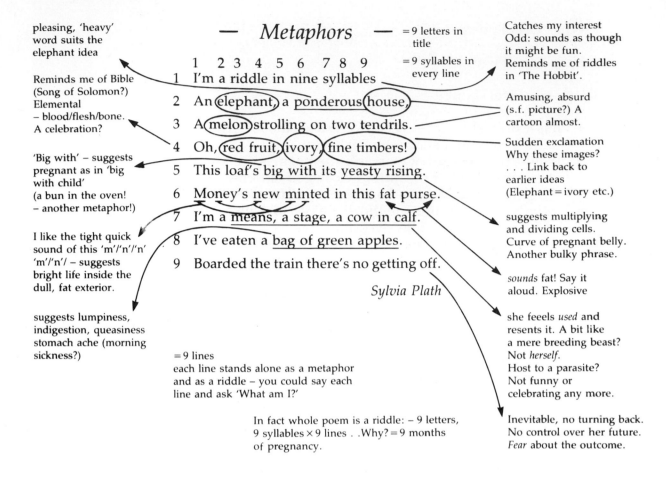

— *Metaphors* —

= 9 letters in title

= 9 syllables in every line

1 2 3 4 5 6 7 8 9

1 I'm a riddle in nine syllables

2 An elephant, a ponderous house,

3 A melon strolling on two tendrils.

4 Oh, red fruit, ivory, fine timbers!

5 This loaf's big with its yeasty rising.

6 Money's new minted in this fat purse.

7 I'm a means, a stage, a cow in calf.

8 I've eaten a bag of green apples.

9 Boarded the train there's no getting off.

Sylvia Plath

pleasing, 'heavy' word suits the elephant idea

Reminds me of Bible (Song of Solomon?) Elemental – blood/flesh/bone. A celebration?

'Big with' – suggests pregnant as in 'big with child' (a bun in the oven! – another metaphor!)

I like the tight quick sound of this 'm'/'n'/'n' 'm'/'n'/ – suggests bright life inside the dull, fat exterior.

suggests lumpiness, indigestion, queasiness stomach ache (morning sickness?)

Catches my interest Odd: sounds as though it might be fun. Reminds me of riddles in 'The Hobbit'.

Amusing, absurd (s.f. picture?) A cartoon almost.

Sudden exclamation Why these images? . . . Link back to earlier ideas (Elephant = ivory etc.)

suggests multiplying and dividing cells. Curve of pregnant belly. Another bulky phrase.

sounds fat! Say it aloud. Explosive

she feeels *used* and resents it. A bit like a mere breeding beast? Not *herself.* Host to a parasite? Not funny or celebrating any more.

Inevitable, no turning back. No control over her future. *Fear* about the outcome.

= 9 lines
each line stands alone as a metaphor and as a riddle – you could say each line and ask 'What am I?'

In fact whole poem is a riddle: – 9 letters, 9 syllables × 9 lines . .Why? = 9 months of pregnancy.

1 What sort of poem is it?

2 How does it work?

3 What do I feel about it?

1 Mixed feelings about pregnancy.

- Begins in detached, half-joking way; something of a game; sees herself as a faintly absurd cartoon figure (lines 1–3).
- Moves to what is almost a joyful, celebratory view of pregnancy (line 4).
- Away from this high point, in lines 4 and 6, doubts begin to creep in with one image in each line positive, the other less so. Physical revulsion sets in.
- Leaves us with an increasing sense of desperation. She feels used, resentful and fearful.

Overall, the powerful negative images with which the poem leaves us prevail, though the other more positive aspects of her pregnancy are still glimpsed through the turmoil.

2 • Primarily through metaphors as the title suggests. Each line is a self-contained metaphor. The structure of the poem with its nine lines and nine syllables per line is itself a metaphor for the nine months of pregnancy.
  • Strong visual images such as 'a melon strolling on two tendrils'.
  • Complex patterns of associations and tight network of images as for example lines 2, 3, 4. Images of heaviness, bulkiness predominate and appear in seven out of nine lines. Strongly physical.
  • Strong emphasis on sounds echoing sense. For example lines 2, 5, 6.
  • It's dramatic, speaks personally and directly to the reader. ('I'm a riddle . . .') and engages interest by its riddling.
  • We share her confusion – it's deliberately disorientating at first reading – and re-enact her emotions as they develop over the nine lines.

3 • After initial uncertainty, a sense of pleasure at having cracked the puzzle. On re-reading a growing sense of dismay and a sharing of her fears coupled with great admiration for the technical skill, the control which allows her to move me through such a range of emotions in so short a space. I don't know the tumultuous mental state of being pregnant: I feel I understand this more now. The poem enlarges my experience.

The poems on the following pages should be approached through the same sequence of activities.

The Sick Rose

O Rose thou art sick.
The invisible worm,
That flies in the night
In the howling storm:

Has found out thy bed
Of crimson joy:
And his dark secret love
Does thy life destroy.

William Blake

— *In a Station of the Metro* —

The apparition of these faces in the crowd;
Petals on a wet, black bough.

Ezra Pound

— *Mirror* —

I am silver and exact. I have no preconceptions.
Whatever I see I swallow immediately
Just as it is, unmisted by love or dislike.
I am not cruel, only truthful –
The eye of a little god, four-cornered.
Most of the time I meditate on the opposite wall.
It is pink, with speckles. I have looked at it so long
I think it is a part of my heart. But it flickers.
Faces and darkness separate us over and over.

Now I am a lake. A woman bends over me,
Searching my reaches for what she really is.
Then she turns to those liars, the candles or the moon.
I see her back, and reflect it faithfully.
She rewards me with tears and an agitation of hands.
I am important to her. She comes and goes.
Each morning it is her face that replaces the darkness.
In me she has drowned a young girl, and in me an old woman
Rises toward her day after day, like a terrible fish.

Sylvia Plath

— *Nothing Gold Can Stay* —

Nature's first green is gold,
Her hardest hue to hold.
Her early leaf's a flower;
But only so an hour.
Then leaf subsides to leaf.
So Eden sank to grief,
So dawn goes down to day.
Nothing gold can stay.

Robert Frost

— *Ballad* —

When lovers have caught fire all over
They hold hands
And together throw themselves
Into a wedding ring
With a little water in it.

It's an important fall in life
And they smile happily
And have their arms full of flowers
And they slide very tenderly
And they slide majestically on foot,
Calling out each other's name in the daytime
And hearing themselves at night.

After a while
Their day and night get mixed up
In a sort of thick sadness. . . .

The wedding ring answers
From the other world.
Over there
Is a big beach
Covered with bones
Which embrace
And sleep in their exhausted whiteness,
Like beautiful shells
Which loved each other all their sea.

Marin Sorescu (trans. by Ted Hughes with
Joana Russell-Gebbett)

— *Sally* —

She was a dog-rose kind of girl:
Elusive, scattery as petals;
Scratchy sometimes, tripping you like briars.
She teased the boys
Turning this way and that, not to be tamed
Or taught any more than the wind.
Even in school the word 'ought' had no meaning
For Sally. On dull days
She'd sit quiet as a mole at her desk
Delving in thought.
But when the sun called
She was gone, running the blue day down
Till the warm hedgerows prickled the dusk
And moths flickered out.

Her mother scolded; Dad
Gave her the hazel-switch,
Said her head was stuffed with feathers
And a starling tongue.
But they couldn't take the shine out of her;
Even when it rained
You felt the sun saved under her skin.
She'd a way of escape
Laughing at you from the bright end of a tunnel,
Leaving you in the dark.

Phoebe Hesketh

— *Men on Allotments* —

As mute as monks, tidy as bachelors,
They manicure their little plots of earth.
Pop music from the council house estate
Counterpoints with the Sunday-morning bells,
But neither siren voice has power for these
Drab solitary men who spend their time
Kneeling, or fetching water, soberly,
Or walking softly down a row of beans.

Like drill-sergeants, they measure their recruits.
The infant sprig receives the proper space
The manly fullgrown cauliflower will need.
And all must toe the line here; stem and leaf,
As well as root, obey the rule of string.
Domesticated tilth aligns itself
In sweet conformity; but head in air
Soars the unruly loveliness of beans.

They visit hidden places of the earth
When tenderly with fork and hand they grope
To lift potatoes, and the round, flushed globes
Tumble like pearls out of the moving soil.
They share strange intuitions, know how much
Patience and energy and sense of poise
It takes to be an onion; and they share
The subtle benediction of the beans.

They see the casual holiness that spreads
Along obedient furrows. Cabbages
Unfurl their veined and rounded fans in joy,
And buds of sprouts rejoice along their stalks.
The ferny tops of carrots, stout red stems
Of beetroot, zany sunflowers with blond hair
And bloodshot faces, shine like seraphim
Under the long flat fingers of the beans.

U. A. Fanthorpe

— *Mare Nostrum* —

Changeable beast with rumpled fur of foam
She plunges along the land,
Held by a moonstring, yet by solid rock
Hardly contained.

She is nothing to look at – only clouds and light
Contrive her vanishing jewels,
Her melting zircon and her solid agate.
If you would see her nature, watch

Those palpitating globes within the pool
More transparent yet more firm than mist:
Her life is a bubble of nothing, cool
Nothing, and like the jellyfish persists.

This yielding overpowers. All in her likeness
Are flutes and whorls in shell and rock and sand,
The conch full of her music,
The water-colours of wentletrap and fan.

And men who chose the shore, aeons ago,
Still spin their memories of her into glass,
Whose splinters worn by water seem to be
Solid green fragments of the sea.

But solid forms renounce her. As for men,
Though other vertebrates return,
Choice of dry land has lost her, let them swim
Each summer through her waves, they never find home.
The lost sea-nature. If her deeps are still,
She has given to men who yearn and may not return to
     them
Only the restless surface,
The quiet buried away,
The sunset shattered across the rocks in spray.

Anne Ridler

— *Fire-eater* —

My father speaking was like conjurors I'd seen
pulling bright silk hankies, scarves, a flag
up out of their innards, red, blue, green,
so many colours it would make me gag.

Dad's eldest brother had a shocking stammer.
Dad punctuated sentence ends with but . . .
Coarser stuff than silk they hauled up grammar
knotted together deep down in their gut.

Theirs are the acts I nerve myself to follow.
I'm the clown sent in to clear the ring.
Theirs are the tongues of fire I'm forced to swallow
then bring back knotted, one continuous string
igniting long-pent silences, and going back
to Adam fumbling with Creation's names;
and though my vocal cords get scorched and black
there'll be a constant singing from the flames.

Tony Harrison

The following poem is written in Creole as is 'Fe Tek a Stride' on p. 17. Look back at what Clive Webster says about Creole and then follow his advice – practise reading the poem aloud before you jot down any notes about it.

— *Wha Fe Call I'* —

Miss Ivy, tell mi supmn,
An mi wan' yuh ansa good.
When yuh eat roun 12 o'clock,
Wassit yuh call yuh food?

For fram mi come yah mi confuse,
An mi noh know which is right,
Weddah dinnah a de food yuh eat midday,
Or de one yuh eat a night.

Mi know sey breakfus a de mawnin one
But cyan tell ef suppa a six or t'ree,
An one ting mi wi nebba undastan,
Is when yuh hab yuh tea.

Miss A dung a London ha lunch 12 o'clock,
An dinnah she hab bout t'ree,
Suppa she hab bout six o'clock,
But she noh hab noh tea.

Den mi go a Cambridge todda day,
Wi habe dinnah roun' bout two,
T'ree hour later mi frien she sey,
Mi hungry, how bout yuh?

Joe sey im tink a suppa time,
An mi sey yes, mi agree,
She halla, 'Suppa? a five o'clock,
Missis yuh mussa mean tea!'

Den Sunday mi employer get up late,
Soh she noh habe breakfus nor lunch,
But mi hear she a talk bout 'Elevenses',
An one sinting dem call 'Brunch'.

Breakfus, elevenses, an brunch,
Lunch, dinnah, suppa, tea,
Mi brain cyan wuk out which is which,
An when a de time fe hab i'.

Mi noh tink mi a badda wid no name,
Mi dis a nyam when time mi hungry,
I or doah mi 'tomach wi glad fe de food,
I' couldn care less whey mi call i'.

Valerie Bloom

— 7 Comparing two — poems

1 THE PROBLEM

You may be asked as part of your coursework or in preparation for an exam to choose two poems on the same topic from a thematic anthology and compare them, or you may be given two unseen poems and asked to write about their similarities and differences. Both tasks can lead to confusion if you do not have a clear idea of how to tackle them. How do you organise your work? Do you write two separate, short essays and put them together? Do you flit back and forth between the poems?

2 PREPARATION

We suggest a four-phase approach:

(i)   Read both poems once for overall sense of theme, treatment and the nature of the relationship between the two poems.
(ii) Reread poem A and make quick jottings on the situation and the nature of the poem, its 'voice', words, images, ideas, feelings, etc. . . . (as in section 4). Reread poem B and do likewise.
(iii) Say what is unique to each poem with brief supporting evidence. No more than three or four lines here to 'capture' each poem.
(iv) List the main points of similarity and difference between the two poems.

3 WRITING UP

This preparation should enable you to structure an essay as follows:

- Opening paragraph, based upon (iii) above, which captures the quality and nature of the two poems.
- Several subsequent paragraphs, based upon (ii) above, which discuss the details you noticed in your reading of the poems. It is usually best to concentrate first on poem A, then on poem B, just as you did in the note-making.
- Final paragraph, based upon (iv) above, which discusses the main points of similarity and difference and, if appropriate, indicates the reasons for your preference of one poem over the other.

4 AN EXAMPLE

Compare the following two poems. Carry out the four-phase preparation *before* you look ahead to our notes.

Read the poems (phase 1)

—— *The Tom-cat* ——

At midnight in the alley
  A Tom-cat comes to wail,
And he chants the hate of a million years
  As he swings his snaky tail.

Malevolent, bony, brindled,
  Tiger and devil and bard,
His eyes are coals from the middle of Hell
  And his heart is black and hard.

He twists and crouches and capers
  And bares his curved sharp claws,
And he sings to the stars of the jungle nights,
  Ere cities were, or laws.

Beast from a world primeval,
  He and his leaping clan,
When the blotched red moon leers over the roofs
  Give voice to their scorn of man.

He will lie on a rug to-morrow
  And lick his silky fur,
And veil the brute in his yellow eyes
  And play he's tame and purr.

But at midnight in the alley
  He will crouch again and wail,
And beat the time for his demon's song
  With the swing of his demon's tail.

Don Marquis

— *Esther's Tomcat* —

Daylong this tomcat lies stretched flat
As an old rough mat, no mouth and no eyes.
Continual wars and wives are what
Have tattered his ears and battered his head.

Like a bundle of old rope and iron
Sleeps till blue dusk. Then reappear
His eyes, green as ringstones: he yawns wide red,
Fangs fine as a lady's needle and bright.

A tomcat sprang at a mounted knight,
Locked round his neck like a trap of hooks
While the knight rode fighting its clawing and bite.
After hundreds of years the stain's there

On the stone where he fell, dead of the tom:
That was at Barnborough. The tomcat still
Grallochs[1] odd dogs on the quiet,   [1] disembowels
Will take the head clean off your simple pullet,

Is unkillable. From the dog's fury,
From gunshot fired point-blank he brings
His skin whole, and whole
From owlish moons of bekittenings

Among ashcans. He leaps and lightly
Walks upon sleep, his mind on the moon
Nightly over the round world of men,
Over the roofs go his eyes and outcry.

Ted Hughes

Notes around the poems (phase 2)

The whole poem reads like an incantation: it has the pace and rhythm of a chant. Line 3 of each verse has extra syllables and more varied musicality.

The cat emerges from a double darkness:- 'wailing' in local setting of the alley

— *The Tom-cat* —

At midnight in the alley
  A Tom-cat comes to wail,
And he chants the hate of a million years
  As he swings his snaky tail.

'hating' in historical setting as a devilish creature with 'snaky tail'

Strong physical presence. — Malevolent, bony, brindled,
Metaphorical presence. — Tiger and devil and bard,
  His eyes are coals from the middle of Hell
  And his heart is black and hard.

melodramatic, piratical, diabolic portrait.

He's a 'primitive' in his movements (l.1), his song (l.3) and his origins (ll. 3 and 4)

He twists and crouches and capers
  And bares his curved sharp claws,
And he sings to the stars of the jungle nights,
  Ere cities were, or laws.

He's an aggressive primitive, threatening the urban with the law of the jungle.

Cat as 'primeval beast' that scorns human civilisation.

Beasts from a world primeval,
  He and his leaping clan,
When the blotched red moon leers over the roofs
  Give voice to their scorn of man.

He's associated with the moon and stars; cosmic world is 'in the know'

↓

Contrast the daytime cat:
'purrs' for 'wails',
'licks + lies' for 'twists + crouches', 'silky fur' for 'bony' + 'sharp claws'

Tame domestic presence masking the brute within.

He will lie on a rug to-morrow
  And lick his silky fur,
And veil the brute in his yellow eyes
  And play he's tame and purr.

↓

But at midnight in the alley
  He will crouch again and wail,
And beat the time for his demon's song
  With the swing of his demon's tail.

Don Marquis

We're left with the diabolic cat again – all the primitive elements – setting, time, sounds and movement.

Who is Esther? Daughter, little girl, woman?
Contrast between female and male principles.

'Hard' sounds, flat, short vowels, uncompromising, suggests toughness.

— Esther's Tomcat —

Interesting rhymes and half rhymes hold it together along with repeated hard consonants. Strong stresses in each line; no clear stress pattern but 4 main ones in each line. No clear rhyme pattern.

Invited to see Tomcat before us: 'this' tomcat. Conversational to some extent.

Daylong this tomcat lies stretched flat
As an old rough mat no mouth and no eyes
Continual wars and wives are what
Have tattered his ears and battered his head.

Like a bundle of old rope and iron
Sleeps till blue dusk. Then reappear
His eyes, green as ringstones: he yawns wide red,
Fangs fine as a lady's needle and bright.

Suggests strength despite being inert.

No pronoun, tough emeralds?
Note *contrast* between these 'fine' images and dull, moth-eaten ones earlier.

Reminds me of ballads 'green', 'red', 'bright', 'lady' – provides link to medieval story in next verse.

A tomcat sprang at a mounted knight
Locked round his neck like a trap of hooks
While the knight rode fighting its clawing and bite.

Suggests tomcat's audacity and strength.

After hundreds of years the stain's there

Conversational tone.
Almost casual killing.
Conversational.

On the stone where he fell, dead of the tom:
That was at Barnborough. The tomcat still
Grallochs' odd dogs on the quiet,
Will take the head clean off your simple pullet,

A story interpolated. Medieval (= the tom has been around for centuries; it's a survivor). Notice all the 't' sounds.

He leaves his mark.

Physical strength;
a suggestion of *magical* power?
Suggests his sexual strength.

Is unkillable. From the dog's fury,
From gunshot fired point-blank he brings
His skin whole, and whole
From owlish moons of bekittenings

'disembowels = tears the guts from; vicious sounding word

Uncompromising flat statement.

Neat let down from grand line to 'ashcan'.
Almost suggests he's *outside* our little world.

Among ashcans. He leaps and lightly
Walks upon sleep, his mind on the moon
Nightly over the round world of men,
Over the roofs go his eyes and outcry.

open ended

Ted Hughes

What is each poem's character? (phase 3)

(i)   'The Tom-cat' is seen as a demonic creature, viz:

- diabolic tail he swings in vss. 1 and 6
- primitive incantation of rhyme and metre of the verses
- associations with darkness of midnight and pre-history
- strong physical presence.

All of this threatens the comfortable, domestic city world.

(ii) 'Esther's Tomcat' has a sense of strength, independence and overwhelming maleness. He's outside the normal laws of nature; a survivor from an older world, drawing his power from a savage past. Yet, for all that, he's still deceptively domestic – he's Esther's tomcat.

Some points of similarity and difference (phase 4)

- Both have the idea that beneath surface appearance exists a violent, cruel nature – something that takes its power from a savage history. Both contrast the domestic cat with the feral beast.
- Although both poems consist of six four-line verses they are formally quite different. Don Marquis's poem is highly organised in terms of metre and rhyme; the verses are self-contained. Ted Hughes's has no regular metrical pattern but is based on four stresses per line which helps the flat, matter-of-fact tone of the poem. There is no regular rhyme pattern but lots of repeated hard consonants, especially the 't' sounds. Also, the verses are often run-on, not self-contained. The form of Marquis's poem dominates the cat; Esther's tomcat will not be controlled.
- Marquis's poem has a chanting tone, song-like, polished, neatly-packaged. The skill of the performance neuters the image of the tom-cat as a threatening devil: he's more of a pantomime figure. Hughes's poem gains a lot from being a series of flat statements; the violence is stronger through the plain, blunt speaking.
- Vs. 1 of Hughes's poem and vs. 5 of Marquis's poem give corresponding pictures yet they're very different. This is where the contrast between the poems shows.

Now try out the approach of the previous pages with the following pairs of poems.

(i)

— *A Negro Woman* —

carrying a bunch of marigolds
   wrapped
     in an old newspaper:
She carries them upright,
   bareheaded,
     the bulk
of her thighs
   causing her to waddle
     as she walks
looking into
   the store window which she passes
     on her way.
What is she
   but an ambassador
     from another world
a world of pretty marigolds
   of two shades
     which she announces
not knowing what she does
   other
     than walk the streets
holding the flowers upright
   as a torch
     so early in the morning.

William Carlos Williams

— *The Fat Black Woman Goes Shopping* —

Shopping in London winter
is a real drag for the fat black woman
going from store to store
in search of accommodating clothes
and de weather so cold

Look at the frozen thin mannequins
fixing her with grin
and de pretty face salesgals
exchanging slimming glances
thinking she don't notice

Lord is aggravating

Nothing soft and bright and billowing
to flow like breezy sunlight
when she walking

The fat black woman curses in Swahili/Yoruba
and nation language under her breathing
all this journeying and journeying

The fat black woman could only conclude
that when it come to fashion
the choice is lean

   Nothing much beyond size 14

Grace Nichols

(ii)

— *The Send-off* —

Down the close, darkening lanes they sang their way
To the siding-shed,
And lined the train with faces grimly gay.

Their breasts were stuck all white with wreath and spray
As men's are, dead.

Dull porters watched them, and a casual tramp
Stood staring hard,
Sorry to miss them from the upland camp.
Then, unmoved, signals nodded, and a lamp
Winked to the guard.

So secretly, like wrongs hushed-up, they went.
They were not ours:
We never heard to which front these were sent.

Nor there if they yet mock what women meant
Who gave them flowers.

Shall they return to beatings of great bells
In wild train-loads?
A few, a few, too few for drums and yells,
May creep back, silent, to village wells
Up half-known roads.

Wilfred Owen

— *Men Who March Away* —

Song of the Soldiers

What of the faith and fire within us
    Men who march away
    Ere the barn-cocks say
    Night is growing grey,
Leaving all that here can win us;
What of the faith and fire within us
    Men who march away?

Is it a purblind prank, O think you,
    Friend with the musing eye,
    Who watch us stepping by
    With doubt and dolorous sigh?
Can much pondering so hoodwink you!
Is it a purblind prank, O think you,
    Friend with the musing eye?

Nay. We well see what we are doing,
    Though some may not see –
    Dalliers as they be –
    England's need are we;
Her distress would leave us rueing:
Nay. We well see what we are doing,
    Though some may not see!

In our heart of hearts believing
    Victory crowns the just,
    And that braggarts must
    Surely bite the dust,
Press we to the field ungrieving,
In our heart of hearts believing
    Victory crowns the just.

Hence the faith and fire within us
    Men who march away
    Ere the barn-cocks say
    Night is growing grey,
Leaving all that here can win us;
Hence the faith and fire within us
    Men who march away.

Thomas Hardy

(iii)

— *To Lucasta,* Going beyond the Seas —

If to be absent were to be
    Away from thee;
  Or that when I am gone,
  You or I were alone;
Then my *Lucasta* might I crave
Pity from blustring winde, or swallowing wave.

But I'le not sigh one blast or gale
    To swell my saile,
  Or pay a teare to swage
  The foaming blew-Gods rage;
For whether he will let me passe
Or no, I'm still as happy as I was.

Though Seas and Land be 'twixt us both,
    Our Faith and Troth,
  Like separated soules,
  All time and space controules:
Above the highest sphere wee meet
Unseene, unknowne, and greet as Angels greet.

So then we doe anticipate
    Our after-fate,
  And are alive i' th' skies
  If thus our lips and eyes
Can speake like spirits unconfin'd
In Heav'n, their earthy bodies left behind.

Richard Lovelace

— *At Parting* —

Since we through war awhile must part
Sweetheart, and learn to lose
Daily use
Of all that satisfied our heart:
Lay up those secrets and those powers
Wherewith you pleased and cherished me these two years:

Now we must draw, as plants would,
On tubers stored in a better season,
Our honey and heaven;
Only our love can store such food.
Is this to make a god of absence?
A new-born monster to steal our sustenance?

We cannot quite cast out lack and pain.
Let him remain – what he may devour
We can well spare:
He never can tap this, the true vein.
I have no words to tell you what you were,
But when you are sad, think, Heaven could give no more.

Anne Ridler

(iv)

— *Richard Cory* —

Whenever Richard Cory went downtown
    We people on the pavement looked at him:
He was a gentleman from sole to crown,
    Clean-favoured and imperially slim.

And he was always quietly arrayed,
    And he was always human when he talked;
But still he fluttered pulses when he said,
    'Good morning,' and he glittered when he walked.

And he was rich – yes, richer than a king –
    And admirably schooled in every grace:
In fine, we thought that he was everything
    To make us wish that we were in his place.

So on we worked and waited for the light,
    And went without the meat, and cursed the bread;
And Richard Cory, one calm summer night,
    Went home and put a bullet through his head.

Edwin Arlington Robinson

— *Richard Cory* —

They say that Richard Cory owns one-half of this old town
With political connections to extend his weight around.
Born into society, a banker's only child
He had everything a man could want; power, grace, and style.

But I work in his factory
And I curse the life I'm living, and I curse my poverty,
And I wish that I could be, O I wish that I could be . . .
    Richard Cory.

The papers print his picture almost everywhere he goes
Richard Cory at the opera, Richard Cory at a show.
And the rumors of his parties and the orgies on his yachts,
O, he surely must be happy with everything he's got.

But I work in his factory
And I curse the life I'm living, and I curse my poverty,
And I wish that I could be, O I wish that I could be . . .
    Richard Cory.

He freely gave to charity; he had the common touch,
And they were grateful for his patronage, and they thanked him very much.
So my mind was filled with wonder when the evening papers read:
'Richard Cory went home last night and put a bullet through his head.'

But I work in his factory
And I curse the life I'm living, and I curse my poverty,
And I wish that I could be, O I wish that I could be . . .
    Richard Cory

Paul Simon

— 8 *Different versions* —

One way to help you to attend to the detail of language, thought and feeling in poetry is to offer a pair of poems written by two different poets who have used as their starting point the same original poem translated from another language.

Below, we have printed two poems entitled 'The Resurrection of Lazarus': both have grown from a single poem in Romanian by Marin Sorescu. The original was translated literally and then the poets D. J. Enright and Michael Longley – neither of whom reads Romanian – independently wrote their different versions from that translation.

In the original Bible story recounted in Chapter 11 of St John's Gospel, two sisters, Martha and Mary, call on Jesus to help their dying brother, Lazarus. By the time Jesus arrives at their home, Lazarus has already been dead four days. The story continues:

32 Then when Mary was come where Jesus was, and saw him, she fell down at his feet, saying unto him, Lord, if thou hadst been here, my brother had not died.

33 When Jesus therefore saw her weeping, and the Jews also weeping which came with her, he groaned in the spirit, and was troubled.

34 And said, Where have ye laid him? They said unto him, Lord, come and see.

35 Jesus wept.

36 Then said the Jews, Behold how he loved him!

37 And some of them said, Could not this man, which opened the eyes of the blind, have caused that even this man should not have died?

38 Jesus therefore again groaning in himself cometh to the grave. It was a cave, and a stone lay upon it.

39 Jesus said, Take ye away the stone. Martha, the sister of him that was dead, saith unto him, Lord, by this time he stinketh: for he hath been *dead* four days.

40 Jesus saith unto her, Said I not unto thee, that, if thou wouldest believe, thou shouldest see the glory of God?

41 Then they took away the stone *from the place* where the dead was laid. And Jesus lifted up *his* eyes, and said. Father, I thank thee that thou hast heard me.

42 And I knew that thou hearest me always: but because of the people which stand by I said *it*, that they may believe that thou hast sent me.

43 And when he thus had spoken, he cried with a loud voice.
Laz-a-rus, come forth.

44 And he that was dead came forth, bound hand and foot with
grave-clothes: and his face was bound about with a napkin. Jesus
saith unto them. Loose him, and let him go.

In pairs or small groups now look at what the two poets made of the
translation of Marin Sorescu's original poem. Read the poems
through to yourself and then listen to them read aloud by someone in
your group.

You will immediately see lots of differences in the two versions. Talk
about these in your groups and think about some of the following:

- On first reading, which version *appeals* more to you?
- Now look more closely at the *language* of the poems. Is the *tone* of
  the two poems different? similar? What makes you think this?
- Is the way in which each poet *interprets* Sorescu's poem similar?
  different? What, in particular, makes you think this?

You can approach the other paired poems in this section in a similar
way, focusing on the poems' appeal, tone, and language and on the
writers' interpretation of the situation. The first two translations are
from a poem by the Russian poet Andrei Voznesensky. These are
followed by two further interpretations of another poem by Marin
Sorescu and by two versions of a poem by W. B. Yeats.

— *The Resurrection of Lazarus* —

What have you done to me, Lord,
Just when I'd managed to loosen up!

It was like having the mist lifted from my eyes
And I was beginning to see the darkness.
Now I realise the moon is different,
The joints of things are different too.

It was like having an opaque plug removed from my ears,
The true song had become clear to me.
You don't know what the secret sounds
Of a thought can mean, as it unfolds.

Now it feels as if someone has clubbed me on the head,
And I'm returning to my old bewilderment.
I hear that you are the one who hurt me so much
When you made the gravestone move aside.

Marin Sorescu (trans. by D. J. Enright with Joana Russell-Gebbett)

— The Resurrection of Lazarus —

God, what have you done to me,
Just when I was beginning to unwind!

It was like having my eyes demystified
And learning to see in the dark.
From a biochemical point of view
I was looking at a different moon.

It was like unmuffling my eardrums
And receiving the song of myself
Loud and clear on all wavelengths.
I made it up as I went along.

Now I feel I've been out for the count
And am coming round, punchdrunk as usual.
You are the burglar, the grave-robber.
You are the one who mugged me.

Marin Sorescu (trans. by Michael Longley with
Joana Russell-Gebbett)

— First Frost —

A girl is freezing in a telephone booth,
huddled in her flimsy coat,
her face stained by tears
and smeared with lipstick.

She breathes on her thin little fingers.
Fingers like ice. Glass beads in her ears.

She has to beat her way back alone
down the icy street.

First frost. A beginning of losses.
The first frost of telephone phrases.

It is the start of winter glittering on her cheek,
the first frost of having been hurt.

— First Ice —

A girl freezes in a telephone booth.
In her draughty overcoat she hides
A face all smeared
In tears and lipstick.

She breathes on her thin palms.
Her fingers are icy. She wears earrings.

She'll have to go home alone, alone,
Along the icy street.

First ice. It is the first time.
The first ice of telephone phrases.

Frozen tears glitter on her cheeks –
The first ice of human hurt.

Andrei Voznesensky
(trans. by George Reavey)

Andrei Voznesensky
(trans. by Stanley Kunitz)

— *Fresco* —

In hell, maximum use
Is made of the sinners.

With the help of tweezers,
Brooches and bracelets, hairpins and rings,
Linen and bedclothes
Are extracted from the heads of the women.
Who are subsequently thrown
Into boiling cauldrons
To keep an eye on the pitch,
And see that it doesn't boil over.

Then some of them
Are transformed into dinner pails
In which hot sins are carried to the domiciles
Of pensioned-off devils.

The men are employed
For the heaviest work,
Except for the hairiest of them,
Who are spun afresh
And made into mats.

Marin Sorescu (trans. by D. J. Enright with
Joana Russell-Gebbett)

— *Fresco* —

They end in Hell
Used up.

We pluck off with tweezers
Everything that served the women's looks:
Their brooches, rings and bracelets,
The pins that skewered their hair.
They lose their linen
We strip the sheets off the beds
They made and lay in and, boiling in pitch,
It is up to the women to see
The cauldrons don't boil over.

Some, if we choose,
Can be dinner-pails and visit thus
Our fat old devils
When they send out for a quart of hot sins.

The men likewise
We work them to a frazzle
All but the hairiest: those we set women unpicking
To make into doormats.

Marin Sorescu (trans. by David Constantine with
Joana Russell-Gebbett)

Two versions of a poem by W. B. Yeats

— *The Old Pensioner* —

I had a chair at every hearth
When no one turned to see,
With 'Look at the old fellow there;
And who may he be?'
And therefore do I wander on,
And the fret lies on me.

The road-side trees keep murmuring.
Ah, wherefore murmur ye,
As in the old days long gone by,
Green oak and poplar tree?
The well-known faces are all gone,
And the fret lies on me.

— *The Lamentation of the Old Pensioner* —

Although I shelter from the rain
Under a broken tree,
My chair was nearest to the fire
In every company
That talked of love or politics,
Ere time transfigured me.

Though lads are making pikes again
For some conspiracy,
And crazy rascals rage their fill
At human tyranny,
My contemplations are of Time
That has transfigured me.

There's not a woman turns her face
Upon a broken tree,
And yet the beauties that I loved
Are in my memory;
I spit into the face of Time
That has transfigured me.

— 9 Making poems: — Writers' and readers' drafts

Whether the task is to write a poem or to read someone else's, with most poems it takes a little time to sort out the words and meanings. Both writers and readers often use notes to help them think through their ideas and feelings, jotting down words and phrases in a random way as their thoughts develop.

This section concentrates on two new poems, 'Paint Box' by Phoebe Hesketh and 'Moonfall' by Colin Rowbotham. In each case we have printed some early drafts (there were several other early versions which we have no room to include) so that you can see how the poem developed towards its final form. With 'Paint Box' we have also given you the annotations of a GCSE student, Marian, as she took her 'mental walk' around the poem (see section 4) and two extracts from her final essay where she said what the ending of the poem meant to her.

Work through the material on 'Paint Box' first, comparing your 'readings' with those of Marian and others in your group. Then look at 'Moonfall', perhaps a more difficult poem, to see how it has been made and how you and other students understand it.

The Paint Box

1   ● With a partner, read through the three versions of the poem below.
    ● On your own, jot down the main changes that you notice.
    ● Take each of the three sections of the final draft in turn and discuss with your partner why you think the changes have been made.

DRAFT 1

— *The Paint Box* —

He tried to tell them what he felt
but the words wouldn't come
till he started to paint
and said it in colours.
White for Sunday morning shading to
grey;

✓
Story - time   (going to bed) was purple
and Monday a bright yellow new week.
Red was shouting in the playground.

Teacher said: 'You must learn to write,'
but he couldn't make spiky As and Ws.
She gave him a painting-book
✓ and pointed to the bird-cage:
? brush / the^{his} colours wouldn't fit the lines
so he made a small brown smudge inside.
'What's that ?' ('That's not a cage,') teacher frowned
and couldn't see that he'd painted himself.

? hand pointed out that the cage was
there printed in the painting-book –
he'd painted something else, so _____

Phoebe Hesketh

DRAFT 2

— *The Paint Box* —

He tried to tell them what he felt
could say it only in colours –
Sunday's white page shading to grey;
story time, purple
and Monday, a bright yellow new week. *morning*
Scarlet was shouting in the playground.

Round as an egg and acorns, his world,
a cocoon.
The schoolroom, squares and angles,
spiked him with letters.
'You must learn to read', they said
and gave him a painting-book alphabet.
Apple swelled beautifully red; balloon
expanding *ed* in blue. *for a bird*
C was a Cage, with a bird, bars
unyielding; his brush wavered through
finding himself
a small brown smudge inside.

C was a cage with canary –
his brush wavered through.

Phoebe Hesketh

FINAL DRAFT

— *Paint Box* —

He tried to tell them what he felt,
could say it only in colours –
Sunday's white page shading to grey
of evening clocks and bells-in-the rain.
Monday morning, bright yellow brass
of a cock crowing.
Story-time, purple.
Scarlet is shouting in the playground.

His world's a cocoon
round as an egg, an acorn
sprouting green.
The schoolroom square and hard;
his desk hard and square
facing the enemy blackboard.

'You must learn to read,' they said
and gave him a painting-book alphabet.
Apple swelled beautifully red. Balloon
expanded in blue.
C was a cage for a bird;
his brush wavered through
painting himself
a small brown smudge inside.

Phoebe Hesketh

2 Now, read Marian's thought-track around the poem. She followed the guide-lines given in section 4, but she had not seen the early drafts of the poem as you have.

- Did you have the same thoughts as she had at any points?
- Where did your ideas differ?

Talk about Marian's first impressions with your partners.

1st thought
during poem – goes through colours in his paintbox, explaining them. 1st + 2nd lines 'talking with colours' suggest an artist

2nd thought
2nd verse- shapes curved and straight-edged. Like 'square + hard'- very abrupt. I think we're talking about children.

— Paint Box —

He tried to tell them what he felt
could say it only in colours –
Sunday's white page shading to grey
of evening clocks and bells-in-the-rain.
Monday morning, bright yellow brass
of a cock crowing.
Story-time, purple.
Scarlet is shouting in the playground.

His world's a cocoon
round as an egg, an acorn
sprouting green.
The schoolroom square and hard;
his desk hard and square
facing the enemy blackboard.

'You must learn to read,' they said
and gave him a painting-book alphabet.
Apple swelled beautifully red. Balloon
expanded in blue.
C was a cage for a bird;
his brush wavered through
painting himself
a small brown smudge inside.

Phoebe Hesketh

6th thought (re-read)
a slow child, trying to express himself going on journey to school. He's inside himself – can't get out 'an egg, acorn' scared of teacher, enemy blackboard can't cope

3rd thought
3rd verse A for apple B for Balloon C for cage etc. Methodical, confusing? 'painting himself as a small brown smudge'. Is this suggesting that he is doing self-portrait or is he painting a smudge for himself?

5th thought
re – 1st verse, colours mentioned – white yellow purple scarlet 2nd verse green 3rd red blue brown

4th thought (re-read)
this is definitely a poem for children, or maybe it's about children? I don't like how it rhymes, uncanny. White Sunday page to start, gradually filling in.

3 Marian then went on to write an essay about the poem for her GCSE folder. Near the beginning she said this about her reading and about her first, second and third 'thoughts'. Read it aloud to your partner.

I must admit the first time I read the poem I was confused. Things didn't quite fall into place and I wasn't even certain I knew what it was about, other than observing lots of colours being mentioned, and linking that to the title. I decided it was the first verse which was throwing me, so I read it again.

Then she went on to talk about the details of the poem and ended with two accounts of the final lines, a literal-minded one and, as an afterthought, a reading that gives her insight into the whole poem. Again, read Marian's comments aloud.

The 3rd verse quotes the teacher dictating 'you must!' which I do not feel is a very understanding attitude. The painting-book alphabet is very methodical. The apple and balloon when coloured, expand and swell, lovely words explaining them getting larger and almost coming alive; for C, the author used cage. I would have preferred to see a cow or a cat, something far simpler for a young child to understand. The closing sentence, 'a small brown smudge inside.' My first thoughts on this were that it was a sentence with two meanings. I opted for in my opinion the correct one after re-reading the line, what Hesketh was trying to conclude was that, although the child was able to develop his ideas in his head, even using colours all he could establish on paper was a brown smudge. I can imagine the frustration of knowing what balloons, apples and cages look like, but being unable to produce a portrait.

An after-thought about the 3rd verse, after commenting on the use of cage for the letter C being inappropriate is that Hesketh used a cage as another way of portraying the feeling of being enclosed and the boy being unable to show his feelings. Also the boy being like a bird in a cage like the child in his classroom – there is no way out, no escape.

- Do you agree with Marian's afterthought?
- Are there any things you want to say about the poem which are not mentioned here?
- If you feel strongly about the poem, or Marian's comments, or both, write about it for your coursework folder.

Moonfall

The writer's 'working' for this poem covers ten pages – a mixture of typed notes, many drafts in verse form and longhand jottings. We have selected four pieces, including the final version, to show you the main stages in the process of composition.

1 First, concentrate on the final version. Read it through to yourself and make your own jottings around the poem (as in section 4).

—— *Moonfall* ——

I never saw you in your prime,
Skymother. A woman of substance
Then, they say; as dense and lucid
As a split flint. Chief mover
At festivities; a guide
To townless folk moonlighting
Across cat-striped sands.

I glimpsed you late last night
As we drove from a party
Where no-one spoke your name. You'd paled
And lost weight (did iron
Sap your magic?) The car swung
In lane and you dropped like an eggshell behind
The massed cartons and brandnames of town.

Colin Rowbotham

Compare notes with a partner and find out what the rest of the class has made of the poem. Try to be as clear as you can about the poem before looking at the drafts.

2 Colin Rowbotham seems to have gone through some fairly distinct phases in making this poem: word-play (draft 1), talking to himself (draft 2), shaping into poem form (draft 3), and the final version. Each draft was composed directly on to the typewriter, with any longhand notes added later.

Now, with a partner, read through each of these earlier drafts in turn, pausing to jot down one or two points that you want to comment on about each draft.

Draft 1   *MOON POEM*

                                          MOONSCAPE

                                          MOONSHOT

Another old story id this is this.
Then id came of age and went to school.
Then they turned to the sun.
Moon and flints that same light inside the jelly egg and little fat women.
Walking down the century museum jumping starting at your reflection on the walls flinching perhaps flinching wincing. winching flensing. fleecing wenching.

Draft 1 ● *Why are all three early titles eventually rejected?*
     ● *What does a 'split flint' (final version) look like?*
     ● *How does it connect with 'jelly egg' and 'little fat women'?*

Draft 2   *MOONSHOT*

1) the moon the stone age women flint the variety. the changes. nomads making their ways by might across catstriped dunes herringstriped dunes.
you were always there you were easy to count you were easy to watch.

so how many stanzas? 3 I think.

first stanza about how impt the moon was. a dartboard to mark our triumphs on. maybe four stanzas.

first stanza about how heavy, seeable, powerful you wre.
second stanza about how I saw you the other night

moon. names: moonshot moonscape luna crescent.

So what's the problem? Basically you've got the one image of you coming home in a car from a party & seeing the moon looking like a halfeggshell behind cloud and then as the car swung round (got in lane) she disappears, shoots down like an eggshell behind the cereal boxes we call the city. Just made you out behind the lights. you must have lost weight.

So, all you need is two stanzas (to the moon? a title? with as many contrasts as possible.

I never saw you in your prime skymother they all looked up to you then. you directed the festivals. weighty heavy you were the centre of attention at festivities, guided the tribes moonlighting from one home to another
no cities then.

I glimpsed you the other night coming from a party where no one had mentioned your name. you'd lost weight. as the car swung around the the roundabout. we call our city.

Draft 2 ● *'So what's the problem?' the writer asks himself. It seems to be partly an organisational one at this stage. How does he sort out his two views of the moon?*

Draft 3   *MOONFALL*

I never saw you in your prime,
Skymother. A woman of substance
Then, they say: as dense and lucid
As a split flint. Chief mover
At festivities; a guide
To townless tribes (folk) moonlighting
Over cat-striped sands.

I glimpsed a bit of you one night,
On a drive-back from a party
Where no-one mentioned you. You'd paled
And   Lost weight (xxxxxxxxxx they say iron
Saps magic). As the car swung
Into lane, you shot – a half-eggshell – behind heaps
Of packaging and

Draft 3 ● *Verse 1 is nearly fixed; verse 2 still has changes to be made.*
     ● *Compare this draft with the final version and ask yourselves about the reasons for the alterations.*

— 10 Coursework — projects

The aim of this section is to suggest a variety of possible approaches to poets and their work that would be suitable for your own individual projects. Whether you undertake such a project for GCSE, Standard Grade or A level, or simply out of personal interest, we hope you will find some useful suggestions.

1 STUDYING A POET'S WORK

Commonly, fifteen or twenty poems by a single author such as R. S. Thomas, Ted Hughes, Seamus Heaney, Sylvia Plath or Stevie Smith are required reading when studying for an exam. Increasingly, students are able to study the work of a poet of their own choosing. In either case, the problem of how to come to terms with a body of poems by one poet has to be faced. How might you find a 'way-in'? Here are a few starting points.

(i)   Reading – in groups

- Groups choose up to three poems on which to concentrate.
- Read each poem silently and aloud. Look for opportunities to use more than one voice per poem.
- An LP recording or cassette tape may be available. Try to hear it.
- Talk about your first impressions of the poems. List any questions that you would like answered.
- Prepare a reading of the poems for the rest of the class. (See (iv) below.)

(ii)   Note-making – on your own

Individually make your own notes around each of the three poems (as in section 4).

(iii)   Sharing impressions – in groups

- Groups pool individual ideas.
  What is each poem about?
  How is it said?
  What feelings does it leave you with?
- List any common themes, attitudes or ways of writing that recur.
  It may help to underline phrases that seem characteristic of this
  poet.

(iv)   Putting ideas together – whole class

- Each group presents the prepared reading (from (i) above) to the
  rest of the class.
- Each group talks about what they have found of interest in this
  poem and, where appropriate, the other two poems.
- Individuals jot down their own notes and ask questions.
- The class should now be able to summarise the main
  characteristics of the poet's writing.
- This may be a good point at which to seek further information
  about the poet from other sources. Questions that it might be
  helpful to ask may be about the circumstances in which the poems
  were written, the period, background setting or the poet's
  personal life.

2 FOCUSING YOUR IDEAS – FOR GROUPS OR INDIVIDUALS

The following activities will help you to a better understanding of a
particular writer's work:

- compiling a folder on the reading you have done, the life and
  background of the poet, what appeal you find in his or her work
  and, perhaps, some of your own poems;
- creating a wall display to capture what you think is the spirit of the
  poet's work;
- making a short taped anthology of the best reading you can make
  of a selection of the poems.

You may want to introduce and link the poems with your own
comments and background information.

On pp. 101–104 you will find a list of books by a wide range of poets
whose work may appeal to you and browsing through them might
form the starting point for such a study.

3 MAKING A POETRY JOURNAL – ON YOUR OWN

Over a period of time – it might be two or three weeks, a term or even a whole year or more – try to keep a poetry journal. Here are some of the things that might go into it:

- Sometimes a poem strikes you on first meeting. Jot down your thoughts and feelings as you read. Try to capture all that you experience.
- Perhaps you have read a poem several times. Now give yourself, say, five minutes, and write. Let your hand follow your pen – see where it takes you.
- Copy out words or phrases or lines that you like, and try to explain why you like them.
- If you like the whole poem, copy it out for your journal.
- Make a list of the questions you have about a poem you like.
- Sometimes we are very moved by a poem that reminds us of a personal experience – something that has happened to us or about which we feel very strongly. If you like, describe that personal association.
- Sometimes words make pictures in our heads. Make a sketch of such a picture, and add the words which created the picture.
- Perhaps a title, or a line, or a feeling gives you an idea for a short story, or a scene in a play, or a poem of your own. Write it.
- If there's a poem you get to know really well, try to answer these questions:
  What interests you about the poem?
  As you reread it, how does your sense of the poem develop?
  Does the whole poem work for you? Say what you like (and perhaps dislike) about it.
- Look back through your entries. 'I like poems which . . .' Can you see any connections between the poems you have chosen to write about?

4 THEMATIC PROJECTS – ON YOUR OWN

Poems by different writers often share the same theme though they may approach it in quite different ways. Different poems that look at the same topic can help each other, sparking off new ideas for us as readers.

- Collect your own anthology of poems sharing a common theme. It might be, for instance, poems about a place or places (cities, the countryside, London, Liverpool, Cardiff, Glasgow . . .) or about school or childhood or growing up; or it may be poems about love or war. It might be a collection of poems by black writers or women poets. It might be a collection of song lyrics. What matters is that you choose them because you like them and can see a common thread linking them together.

- Write about your reasons for choosing them and about how they help you think about the theme they all share.
- You could jot notes on each of the poems in your selection.

5 AN ANTHOLOGY FOR OTHER AUDIENCES – FOR GROUPS OR INDIVIDUALS

Linked to the last suggestion and perhaps developing out of it, is the idea of creating a collection of poems suitable for a particular group or situation.

- Choose your own anthology of poems for another class in the school, for a younger year group, for the local primary school or for an assembly. The poems don't have to be linked by a common theme though you may find this helps.
- Write suitable comments to link your chosen poems together into a coherent presentation.
- Present your anthology collection to your chosen audience. Some ways of doing this could be:
  - perform it live with different voices sharing the reading and the linking passages;
  - tape-record it as a radio programme with introduction, links and suitable music;
  - present it as a set of poster poems to be displayed on the classroom wall;
  - when you have achieved your finished product, whatever form it takes, write about what you chose to include and why. Write about the problems and pleasures of creating and presenting your anthology.

6 CREATIVE RESPONSES – ON YOUR OWN

Although we may discuss poems, criticise them and perform them, sometimes we are prompted to respond in a different way by writing our own original poem or story or by drawing a picture to illustrate the piece. Elizabeth wrote the following poem when she was about sixteen as her own response to Sylvia Plath's poem 'Mirror' which you will find on p. 48.

— *Lines* —

(after Mirror, Sylvia Plath)

The human face
Is the individual's album;
Showing the joys, the heartaches
The sadness and the laughter.
Each line is a memory,
Happy or not,
Of a time long gone by
Of a person or a place.
Perhaps it is the sadness
Of these memories
That makes us hate these lines.

Perhaps it is the happiness
– of now and years to come –
That makes us cry dry sobs and
Long
For days of youth
Into the mirror of our hearts.

Elizabeth Noble

A totally different creative response to a poem is a drawing such as
Kristina's illustration (opposite) to Voznesensky's poem 'First Ice'
(p. 68) the opening lines of which read:

A girl freezes in a telephone booth.
In her draughty overcoat she hides
A face all smeared
In tears and lipstick . . .

- Over a period of time, aim to build up a small selection of poems
  with your own creative responses (poems, stories, or pictures).
- You may wish to write an accompanying commentary explaining
  what it was in the original poem that triggered your response and
  what it was you were trying to capture in your own poems,
  pictures or stories.
- If you are not confident about your drawing, there's no reason
  why you shouldn't cut out images from magazines and
  newspapers, creating a collage effect around the original poem or
  your own writing. You could equally well write about why you
  chose those particular images and why you think they are
  appropriate.

First Ice
Kristina Nuttall

7 PARODY AND PASTICHE – ON YOUR OWN OR IN PAIRS

There's a saying that 'imitation is the sincerest form of flattery' and certainly poets have imitated each other's work for generations, sometimes seriously and sometimes with the intention of poking fun. A serious attempt to adopt the style of a writer is called **pastiche** (rather as paste jewellery looks just like the real thing); a lighthearted mockery of a writer's style intended to entertain is a **parody** or a **burlesque**. Either of these forms can be fun to try and attempting them can help you very quickly to understand how a particular poet writes and achieves certain effects. D. H. Lawrence's long poem 'Snake' is well known. The opening lines

> A snake came to my water-trough
> On a hot, hot day, and I in pyjamas for the heat,
> To drink there.

become, in fifteen year old Steven's pastiche version,

> A hedgehog came to my garden
> On a hot, humid day
> To eat the vegetation there . . .

and continues in the same vein for thirty lines. He may not be too well-informed on the feeding habits of hedgehogs but he does capture something of the tone and movement of Lawrence's verse.

Similarly, Wendy Cope parodies Shakespeare's Sonnet 55 which begins

> Not marble nor the gilded monuments
> Of princes shall outlive this pow'rful rhyme;
> But you shall shine more bright in these contents
> Than unswept stone, besmear'd with sluttish time.

Her version starts:

> Not only marble but the plastic toys
> From cornflake packets will outlive this rhyme:
> I can't immortalize you love – our joys
> Will lie unnoticed in the vault of time.

- Attempt a poem or a small collection of your own poems – serious or lighthearted – in the style of a writer or writers whose work interests you.
- Say what you found trickiest and/or most satisfying about the exercise.

8 MAPPING YOUR RESPONSES OVER TIME – ON YOUR OWN

Over several months – certainly over the length of your course – you will probably undertake a number of written exercises on different poems. If you have used some of the techniques suggested in this book you may have mapped your readings of poems as we have suggested on pp. 24 and 29 in section 4. An interesting project would be to collect your various responses over time and to reflect on your own development as a reader of poetry.

- How have you changed as a reader of poetry since you began your course?
- Are you more or less confident than when you began?
- Has what appeals to you changed?
- Have group discussion of poems and jotting down notes around the poem been of help to you in getting to grips with particular poems?
- Try to step back from your work and make an assessment of your progress as a reader of poetry in recent months. (Keeping a poetry journal – see above – might be useful here.)
- You may find enough of interest in this exercise for it to provide a topic for discussion in oral assessment.

— 11 Writing for an — examiner

Questions on poems vary from one examination board to another. You may be asked in very general terms to write an essay about an unseen poem, or you may be required to answer a list of comprehension questions about specific details.

We make no attempt to cover all the possibilities. Rather we concentrate upon the following examples:

(i) because they reflect our emphasis upon personal response throughout this book; and

(ii) because if you adopt this approach it provides a good grounding from which you can tackle examination questions which direct you to more particular aspects of a poem.

Here is a poem printed with the instructions from the examiner exactly as it appeared on the examination paper:

Read through the following poem at least once, to get the sense of it.

Born Yesterday

Tightly folded bud,
I have wished you something
None of the others would:
Not the usual stuff
About being beautiful,
Or running off a spring
Of innocence or love –
They will all wish you that,
And should it prove possible,
Well, you're a lucky girl.
But if it shouldn't, then
May you be ordinary;
Have like other women
An average of talents:
Not ugly, not good-looking,
Nothing uncustomary
To pull you off your balance,
That, unworkable in itself,
Stops all the rest from working.

In fact, may you be dull –
If that is what a skilled,
Vigilant, flexible,
Unemphasised, enthralled
Catching of happiness is called.

Philip Larkin

We all wish a newly-born child (a 'tightly folded bud') happiness in life – but what *is* happiness in life? Read the poem again now, feeling and thinking your way carefully into it, and see what different views on the matter you find there. What exactly is Philip Larkin's own feeling about it? What is there in the language of the poem that helps you to share in that feeling? With the help of these questions, say what you yourself feel about 'Born Yesterday' *as a poem*.

- Keep in mind what we have said about reading ('with the eye' and 'with the ear') and note-making ('around the poem').
- Remember how we shaped notes into an essay pattern (section 6, p. 41).

Now, go through the process of reading, note-making and essay-writing for yourself *before* you compare your work with that of the student below. Elizabeth (who was 15 years old at the time) wrote her essay in about forty minutes. She had not seen the poem before.

Elizabeth's essay (uncorrected)

Our comments

'*Born Yesterday*' Philip Larkin

This is a joyful poem covering up a sad man. If you look at the poem superficially, without examining the thoughts behind it, it appears to be a simple, well thought out wish by a kind god parent for his newborn godchild, but to look at the poem deeper uncovers a man who appears to be sad and vulnerable, as well as confused.

Larkin's poem invites us to think directly about the writer's feelings. Elizabeth sees this straight away – 'This is a joyful poem covering up a sad man'. In a simple statement she gets to what she sees as the heart of the poem.

He begins, slightly awed by the baby he is holding;

She begins to show us *how* she gets to the heart of the poem.

'Tightly folded bud'

This is a beautiful line, conjuring up the image of a womb-creased 'scrunched-up' baby. It is tense and stiff in his hands like all new born babies are. The reference to a bud has two meanings to me. It is natural, and like a flower waiting to bloom the image of a bud promises a delightful change; a complete metamorphis.

She responds personally, not by simply saying 'This is a beautiful line' but also by showing what it means *to her*, . . . what associations it has.

The poet is cynical, making fun of other people who wish the baby beauty, innocence etc. He feels it is ironic that these people wish the baby the very things he feels are bound to make them unhappy. At the end of the first verse he says that if the things others wish her come true then:

'Well, you're a lucky girl'

But in the next verse he directly contradicts himself by saying that
he would consider her unlucky or unfortunate to have these traits.

The whole poem centres around his attitude towards his fellows and his realization of the differences between 'others' and himself. He honestly believes that true happines stems from being completely and utterly ordinary and unnoticeable, almost invisible; the kind of person who is never noticed on the street and has no special features or talents.

'Nothing uncustomary to pull you off your balance.'
To him life and happiness should be even, steady, balanced.

His idea of happiness is strange as well. He has designed, created, in the last four lines and ideal, perfect emotion. It is what he would *like* to feel. He thinks it is 'skillful' and 'vigilant'. This implies it must be tended and nurtured if it is to survive; it is not a natural thing for him. It must be a constant surprise and cause 'joy anew' and it must allow freedom. But still he gets back to this overwhelming obsession of his:

'Unemphasised . . . happiness'

Perhaps he feels that if your joy is evident and apparent someone will endeavour to take it away from you.

This man is not happy. There is an underlying sadness within him that he expresses through his dry cynicism. Perhaps to express it directly would be to reveal too much of himself, to be vulnerable; unprotected. This poet has never been ordinary. He has always been

Does she get this right? Does Larkin think that she would be unlucky or unfortunate to have these traits – or, simply, that it is unlikely that it would prove possible?
She doesn't clearly state what he *does* in fact wish for the child ('an average of talents') and the reasons why – i.e. excess in one direction makes life 'unworkable' and 'stops all the rest from working'.

She perceives that the poem focuses every bit as much on Larkin as on the baby and that he values his difference from the norm while wishing the baby a balanced even dull existence. (There's an irony here, isn't there? – How far is *he* aware of it?) She is sensitive to the tone and voice of the poem.

A deeply thoughtful response to Larkin's view of happiness. She seeks out the implications of every word – 'skilful', 'vigilant', etc. . . . . She is concerned, as poets are, with what particular words actually mean.

A thoughtful and justifiable speculation that goes beyond the poem but acknowledges that 'we have no way of knowing' from the words on the page how true it may be.

different; a freak maybe even bullied or ostrecized(?) He would like to be ordinary. It could be his talent for poetry that has made him unhappy; it could be anything. We have no way of knowing. We are left with a sense of sadness, and of sympathy for Philip Larkin but it is touching – what he has written and felt for his godchild is a moving, sensitive insight into his inner thoughts. We feel honoured that he has allowed us to see into his head.

Where Elizabeth might have said more:

> She didn't really get to grips with the *language* of the poem though she felt its effects all right. We would have been interested to see something on the almost conversational tone: 'not the usual stuff' . . . , 'well, you're a lucky girl'; in fact, after the first three lines (with their rhyming 'bud'/'would') everything is deliberately 'non-poetic', in any flowery sense of the word. After the colon in line 3, Larkin's poetic skill, echoing the sense of the poem, goes into hiding. Everything becomes apparently flat and ordinary but the lines are given life by a careful use of stress and half-rhyme ('then'/'women'; 'talents'/'balance'; 'ordinary'/'uncustomary'). He uses a rhymed couplet at the end to close the poem formally.

> The title is worth a second thought. The baby was 'born yesterday' but when adults say 'I wasn't born yesterday' they mean they are not to be taken in. Does this relate to the poem?

Here are some examples of poetry questions from different examination boards for you to work on.

1 FROM LONDON AND EAST ANGLIAN GROUP GCSE, ENGLISH LITERATURE

SECTION A – POETRY
You must answer the whole of Section A.

You are advised to spend about ten minutes reading both of the poems before you write your answers.

Now read the poem Growing Pain *and then do the written work which follows.*

The directions are divided into three sections to help you write about some of the important ideas and feelings in the poem, and about the language.

POEM 1

Growing Pain *Vernon Scannell*

The boy was barely five years old.
We sent him to the little school
And left him there to learn the names
Of flowers in jam jars on the sill
And learn to do as he was told.   5
He seemed quite happy there until
Three weeks afterwards, at night,
The darkness whimpered in his room.
I went upstairs, switched on his light,
And found him wide awake, distraught,   10
Sheets mangled and his eiderdown
Untidy carpet on the floor.
I said, 'Why can't you sleep? A pain?'
He snuffled, gave a little moan,
And then he spoke a single word: 15
'Jessica.' The sound was blurred.
'Jessica? What do you mean?'
'A girl at school called Jessica,
She hurts –' he touched himself between
The heart and stomach '– she has been   20
Aching here and I can see her'.
Nothing I had read or heard
Instructed me in what to do.
I covered him and stroked his head.
'The pain will go, in time,' I said.   25

The Boy
Write about the boy. You may wish to consider the following:

– the problem that prevented him from sleeping;
– the words or phrases used to convey to you his disturbed state of mind;
– why he is so upset.

The Parent
Write about the father. You may wish to consider the following:

– the father's attitude towards his son and towards school in the first part of
  the poem;
– his reaction to his son's problem;
– any change in his attitude caused by the experience.

The Poem
Write about the poem. You may wish to consider the following:

– any phrases, lines or ideas which you feel are interesting;

– how the ones that you select have helped to convey the feeling of the poem
   or have helped you to understand what the poet is trying to explain;
– your views about the way the poet has expressed himself.

Now read the second poem, A Child Half-Asleep, *which also takes as its starting point a child disturbed from sleep. Then do the written work set out below.*

POEM 2

A Child Half-Asleep *Tony Connor*

Stealthily parting the small-hours silence,
a hardly-embodied figment of his brain
comes down to sit with me
as I work late.
Flat-footed, as though his legs and feet
were still asleep.

On the stool,
staring into the fire,
his dummy dangling.

Fire ignites the small coals of his eyes;
it stares back through the holes
into his head, into the darkness.

I ask what woke him.

'A wolf dreamed me,' he says.

Write a brief account of the situation in this poem, and say what you think
has interested the poet.

Compare this poem to 'Growing Pain'. Show how the two poems are similar
or different in their form, tone and language. Include an opinion on each
poem.

2 FROM WELSH JOINT EDUCATION COMMITTEE, GCSE ENGLISH LITERATURE

Manwatching

From across the party I watch you,
Watching her.
Do my possessive eyes
Imagine your silent messages?
5   I think not.
She looks across at you
And telegraphs her flirtatious reply.
I have come to recognize this code,
You are on intimate terms with this pretty stranger,
10   And there is nothing I can do,
My face is calm, expressionless,
But my eyes burn into your back,
While my insides shout with rage.
She weaves her way towards you,
15   Turning on a bewitching smile.
I can't see your face, but you are mesmerised I expect.
I can predict you: I know this scene so well,
Some acquaintance grabs your arm,
You turn and meet my accusing stare head on,
20   Her eyes follow yours, meet mine,
And then slide away, she understands,
She's not interested enough to compete.
It's over now.
She fades away, you drift towards me,
25   'I'm bored' you say, without a trace of guilt,
So we go.
Passing the girl in the hall.
'Bye' I say frostily,
I suppose
30   You winked.

Georgia Garrett

The poet is writing about a girl's thoughts and feelings about her boyfriend at a party.

(a)   Read lines 1–7. What does the girl notice about her boy friend at the party? [3]

(b)   On line 9 she calls the girl she is watching 'this pretty stranger'. What do you think are her real feelings about the girl her boy friend 'watches'? Support your answer with evidence from the poem. [4]

(c)   Choose 3 or 4 words or phrases that give you a vivid impression of how the girl's feeling about her boy friend. Write about them.

Here are two examples of choices you might make. Use them if you wish but feel free to choose any other words or phrases from the poem in your answer:
    'my possessive eyes' (line 3);
    'my eyes burn into your back,
    While my insides shout with rage.' (lines 12–13) [8]

(d)   You are the girl's boy friend. Write what you thought and felt at the party about your girl friend and the other girl. [5]

---

3 FROM LONDON AND EAST ANGLIAN GROUP, GCSE ENGLISH LITERATURE

In the poem which follows, Ted Hughes describes a stag hunt in Devonshire, and contrasts the behaviour of the human beings taking part with that of the animal.

The Stag

While the rain fell on the November woodland shoulder of Exmoor
While the traffic jam along the road honked and shouted
Because the farmers were parking wherever they could
And scrambling to the bank-top to stare through the tree-fringe
Which was leafless,   5
The stag ran through his private forest.

While the rain drummed on the roofs of the parked cars
And the kids inside cried and daubed their chocolate and fought
And mothers and aunts and grandmothers
Were a tangle of undoing sandwiches and screwed-round gossiping   10
   heads
Steaming up the windows,
The stag loped through his favourite valley.

While the blue horsemen down in the boggy meadow
Sodden nearly black, on sodden horses,   15
Spaced as at a military parade,
Moved a few paces to the right and a few to the left and felt rather
   foolish
Looking at the brown impassable river,
The stag came over the last hill of Exmoor.   20

While everybody high-kneed it to the bank-top all along the road
Where steady men in oilskins were stationed at binoculars,
 And the horsemen by the river galloped anxiously this way and that
And the cry of hounds came tumbling invisibly with their echoes down
   through the draggle of trees,   25
Swinging across the wall of dark woodland,
The stag dropped into a strange country.

And turned at the river
Hearing the hound-pack smash the undergrowth, hearing the
    bell-note   30
Of the voice that carried all the others,
Then while his limbs all cried different directions to his lungs, which
    only wanted to rest,
The blue horsemen on the bank opposite
Pulled aside the camouflage of their terrible planet.   35

And the stag doubled back weeping and looking for home up a
    valley and down a valley
While the strange trees struck at him and the brambles lashed him,
And the strange earth came galloping after him carrying the loll-tongued
    hounds to fling all over him   40
And his heart became just a club beating his ribs and his own hooves
    shouted with hounds' voices,
And the crowd on the road got back into their cars
Wet-through and disappointed.

Ted Hughes

Write as fully as you can about the poem, and about the feelings it arouses in you. You may find it helpful to consider the following topics, together with any ideas of your own.

The stag:
    the ways it behaves, and how it seems to feel
        – in the first four verses
        – in the last two verses.

The human beings:
    the different kinds of spectators
    what they do
    how they feel about what they are watching.

The form of the poem:
    any patterns which you notice in the way the poem is written.
    (Try to suggest why you think the poet has used these patterns.)

The language used by the poet:
    any words, phrases or lines which stand out particularly.
    (Try to say why you find them effective.)

Your own feelings:
    try to trace the ways in which your feelings change as you read through
    the poem.

4 FROM AEB GCE A LEVEL ENGLISH LITERATURE

Write a critical appreciation of the following poem, paying attention to such matters as subject, form and style.

July The Seventh

Drugged all day, the summer
Flagged in its heat, brutal
Weather sullen as brass.
There was no comfort in darkness.
Hotter than breath we lay

On beds too warm for moving,
Near open windows. Full of
Spaces the house was, walls
Fretting for a brisk air.
A door slammed flat in its

Loud frame, banging us awake.
Wind was bringing in the storm.
Quick switches of whipped light
Flicked the rooftops, made shadowless
The ends of rooms. The stopped clock

Marked the lightning. I got up
Heavily, shut the house against
Thunder. Rain was a long time
Coming, then sparse drops, stinging
Like metal, hit the bricks, the hot

Pavements. When it sweetened
To plenty, the streets tamed it,
Flowed it in pipes and conduits,
Channelled it underground through
Stony runnels. The rain brought

So faint a smell of hay I searched
My mind for it, thinking it memory.
I lay freshly awake on the cool sheets,
Hearing the storm. Somewhere, far off,
Cut grass lay in files, the hay spoiling.

Leslie Norris
[22]

---

5 FROM AEB GCE A LEVEL ENGLISH, ALTERNATIVE SYLLABUS

Read the following passage:

One summer evening (led by her)* I found   * Nature
A little boat tied to a willow tree
Within a rocky cave, its usual home.

Straight I unloosed her chain, and stepping in
Pushed from the shore. It was an act of stealth
And troubled pleasure, nor without the voice
Of mountain-echoes did my boat move on;
Leaving behind her still, on either side,
Small circles glittering idly in the moon,
Until they melted all into one track
Of sparkling light. But now, like one who rows,
Proud of his skill, to reach a chosen point
With an unswerving line, I fixed my view
Upon the summit of a craggy ridge,
The horizon's utmost boundary; far above
Was nothing but the stars and the grey sky.
She was an elfin pinnace;† lustily   † a small boat
I dipped my oars into the silent lake,
And, as I rose upon the stroke, my boat
Went heaving through the water like a swan;
When, from behind that craggy steep till then
The horizon's bound, a huge peak, black and huge,
As if with voluntary power instinct
Upreared its head. I struck and struck again,
And growing still in stature the grim shape
Towered up between me and the stars, and still,
For so it seemed, with purpose of its own
And measured motion like a living thing,
Strode after me. With trembling oars I turned,
And through the silent water stole my way
Back to the covert of the willow tree;
There in her mooring-place I left my bark,
And through the meadows homeward went, in grave
And serious mood; but after I had seen
That spectacle, for many days, my brain
Worked with a dim and undetermined sense
Of unknown modes of being; o'er my thoughts
There hung a darkness, call it solitude
Or blank desertion. No familiar shapes
Remained, no pleasant images of trees,
Of sea or sky, no colours of green fields;
But huge and mighty forms, that do not live
Like living men, moved slowly through the mind
By day, and were a trouble to my dreams.

Wordsworth is here describing an adventure he had during his childhood.
Examine the passage carefully, tracing the feelings which the author
conveys to us and pointing out some of the ways in which his techniques of
writing make those feelings and the atmosphere clear to the reader. You
should consider such things as tone, rhythm, vocabulary and imagery.

CHECKLIST

Dos

- Do read the poem several times both with the eye and ear – even if you have to mouth it quietly to yourself in order to hear it aloud.
- Do use writing (i.e. jottings) to help you develop your thoughts. Few people can hold all the details of what they want to say in their heads and write an essay straight off without notes.
- Do give the poet the benefit of any doubts you may have until you have really got to grips with his or her poem. It's very rare for examiners to set trivial poems.
- Do be positive and look for the 'plus' points as well as any criticisms you may have.
- Do tolerate puzzling bits. You don't have to be able to paraphrase everything – some lines may remain elusive.
- Do comment fully on particular lines that appeal to you – you'll write best about the parts of the poem that you like.

Don'ts

- Don't fake a response, i.e. by telling the examiner what you *think* he or she wants to hear rather than what you really think and feel yourself.
- Don't be afraid to use the first person when it feels appropriate.
- Don't assume that you have to be either 'for' or 'against' a poem. If you dislike the poem you're probably best advised to avoid the question; there's little purpose in listing a lot of negative points.
- Don't quote lines or phrases simply to let them speak for themselves. Make them work for their place in your essay.
- Don't simply say that you like a line or phrase or that 'it's beautiful' and leave it at that. Say why.
- Don't assume the poem has to have a hidden meaning, that it's a mystery you have to solve. When you have read 'with eye and ear' and thought around the poem, trust your judgement.

— *Dear Mr Lee* —

Dear Mr Lee (Mr Smart says
it's rude to call you Laurie, but that's
how I think of you, having lived with you
really all year), Dear Mr Lee
(Laurie) I just want you to know
I used to hate English, and Mr Smart
is roughly my least favourite person,
and as for Shakespeare (we're doing him too)
I think he's a national disaster, with all those jokes
that Mr Smart has to explain why they're jokes,
and even then no one thinks they're funny,
And T. Hughes and P. Larkin and that lot
in our anthology, not exactly a laugh a minute,
pretty gloomy really, so that's why
I wanted to say Dear Laurie (sorry) your book's
the one that made up for the others, if you
could see my copy you'd know it's lived
with me, stained with Coke and Kitkat
and when I had a cold, and I often
take you to bed with me to cheer me up
so Dear Laurie, I want to say sorry,
I didn't want to write a character-sketch
of your mother under headings, it seemed
wrong somehow when you'd made her so lovely,
and I didn't much like those questions
about *social welfare in the rural community*
and *the seasons as perceived by an adolescent*,
I didn't think you'd want your book
read that way, but bits of it I know by heart,
and I wish I had your uncles and your half-sisters
and lived in Slad, though Mr Smart says your view
of the class struggle is naïve, and the examiners
won't be impressed by me knowing so much by heart,
they'll be looking for terse and cogent answers
to their questions, but I'm not much good at terse and cogent,
I'd just like to be like you, not mind about being poor,
see everything bright and strange, the way you do,
and I've got the next one out of the Public Library,
about Spain, and I asked Mum about learning
to play the fiddle, but Mr Smart says Spain isn't
like that any more, it's all Timeshare villas
and Torremolinos, and how old were you
when you became a poet? (Mr Smart says for anyone
with my punctuation to consider poetry as a career
is enough to make the angels weep).

PS   Dear Laurie, please don't feel guilty for
me failing the exam, it wasn't your fault,
it was mine, and Shakespeare's,
and maybe Mr Smart's, I still love *Cider*,
it hasn't made any difference.

U. A. Fanthorpe

— 12 Resources —

WIDER READING – POETRY BOOKBOXES

All literature courses encourage further reading and many include a section called 'open study' or 'wider reading'. The aim here is to help you with this topic by providing a selected list of books that will extend your reading and from which you could develop the projects outlined in section 9.

Ideally, these books would form the nucleus of a small poetry collection in a school or college English Department, library or resources area. Housed in several LP record cases so that it is easy to transport, such a selection of slim volumes offers the single most valuable resource for work with poetry. Even if you do not have access to a collection, you should be able to obtain any of these books easily; virtually all of them are in paperback editions.

The books have been arranged in three groups:

1 A chronological list of poets from the seventeenth century up to World War II. (Although some of the twentieth century poets in this section continued writing after World War II, they are placed in the period with which they are generally associated.)

2 An alphabetical list of post-war poets.

3 A selection of anthologies.

1 Poets from the seventeenth to the twentieth centuries

William Shakespeare	*The Sonnets*	Penguin
ed. Helen Gardner	*The Metaphysical Poets* (particularly poems of Donne, Herbert, Marvell, Vaughan which are also available in separate Penguin volumes)	Penguin
ed. Douglas Grant	*Pope*	Penguin
William Blake	*Songs of Innocence and Experience,* illuminated edition	OUP
William Wordsworth	*Selected Poems of Wordsworth,* World's Classics edition	OUP

S. T. Coleridge	*The Rime of the Ancient Mariner,* illustrated G. Doré	Dover/Constable
John Keats	*The Poetical Works of John Keats,* World's Classics	OUP
ed. David Wright	*English Romantic Verse*	Penguin
ed. George Macbeth	*Victorian Verse*	Penguin
Thomas Hardy	*Selected Shorter Poems of Thomas Hardy,* ed. J. Wain	Macmillan
G. Manley Hopkins	*Poems and Prose of G. Manley Hopkins,* ed. W. H. Gardner	Penguin
Emily Dickinson	*A Choice of Emily Dickinson's Verse,* ed. Ted Hughes	Faber
W. B. Yeats	*Collected Poems*	Macmillan
ed. Brian Gardner	*Up the Line to Death: The War Poets 1914–18*	Methuen
T. S. Eliot	*Selected Poems*	Faber
D. H. Lawrence	*Selected Poems*	Penguin
Robert Graves	*Selected Poems*	Penguin
Edward Thomas	*Selected Poems*	Faber
Robert Frost	*Selected Poems*	Penguin
Walter de la Mare	*Selected Poems*	Faber
William Carlos Williams	*Selected Poems,* ed. Charles Tomlinson	Penguin
e.e.cummings	*Selected Poems 1923–1958*	Penguin
ed. Robin Skelton	*Poetry of the Thirties*	Penguin
W. H. Auden	*Selected Poems*	Penguin
Dylan Thomas	*Collected Poems*	Dent
ed. Brian Gardner	*The Terrible Rain: The War Poets 1939–45*	Methuen

2 Poets published since 1945, listed alphabetically by author

Anna Adams	*Dear Vincent*	Littlewood Press
Fleur Adcock	*The Incident Book*	OUP
John Agard	*Mangoes and Bullets*	Pluto Press
Maya Angelou	*And Still I Rise*	Virago
Connie Bensley	*Moving In*	Peterloo Poets
James Berry	*Chain of Days*	OUP
John Betjeman	*The Best of Betjeman,* ed. J. Guest	Penguin
Elizabeth Bishop	*Selected Poems*	Chatto & Windus
Valerie Bloom	*Touch Mi: Tell Mi*	Bogle L'Ouverture
Charles Causley	*Collected Poems 1951–1975*	Macmillan
Gillian Clarke	*Selected Poems*	Carcanet
Tony Connor	*Poems With Love Somehow*	OUP
Wendy Cope	*Making Cocoa for Kingsley Amis*	Faber

Jeni Couzyn	*Life By Drowning: Selected Poems*	Bloodaxe
Douglas Dunn	*Selected Poems 1964–83*	Faber
Gavin Ewart	*The Young Pobble's Guide to His Toes*	Hutchinson
U. A. Fanthorpe	*Selected Poems*	Penguin
Elaine Feinstein	*Some Unease and Angels: Selected Poems*	Hutchinson
Lawrence Ferlinghetti	*A Coney Island of Mind*	New Directions and Hutchinson
Thom Gunn	*Selected Poems by Thom Gunn and Ted Hughes*	Faber
Tony Harrison	*Selected Poems*	Penguin
Seamus Heaney	*Selected Poems*	Penguin
Adrian Henri	in *New Volume*	Penguin
Phoebe Hesketh	*Netting the Sun: New and Collected Poems*	Enitharmon Press
Miroslav Holub	*Selected Poems*	Penguin
Ted Hughes	*Selected Poems 1957–81*	Faber
Kathleen Jamie	*The Way We Live*	Bloodaxe
Elizabeth Jennings	*Collected Poems*	Carcanet
Amryl Johnson	*Long Road to Nowhere*	Virago
Linton Kwesi Johnson	*Inglan is a Bitch*	Race Today
Jenny Joseph	*The Thinking Heart*	Secker
James Kirkup	*The Prodigal Son*	OUP
Philip Larkin	*Collected Poems*, ed. A. Thwaite	Marvell/Faber
Laurie Lee	*Selected Poems*	Penguin
Denise Levertov	*Selected Poems*	Bloodaxe
Liz Lochhead	*Dreaming Frankenstein and Other Poems*	Polygon
Robert Lowell	*Selected Poems*	Faber
George MacBeth	*Collected Poems 1958–70*	Macmillan
Norman MacCaig	*Voice Over*	Chatto
Roger McGough	*In The Glassroom* (see also Michael Rosen below)	Jonathan Cape
Don Marquis	*Archy and Mehitabel*	Faber
Adrian Mitchell	*For Beauty Douglas: Collected Poems 1953–79*	Allison & Busby
Grace Nichols	*The Fat Black Woman's Poems*	Virago
Norman Nicholson	*Selected Poems*	Faber
Gareth Owen	*Song of the City*	Fontana Lions
Brian Patten	in *New Volume*	Penguin
Stef. Pixner	*Sawdust and White Spirit*	Virago
Sylvia Plath	*Collected Poems*	Faber
Kathleen Raine	*Collected Poems 1953–80*	Allen & Unwin
Craig Raine	*A Martian Sends A Postcard Home*	OUP
Peter Redgrove	in *Penguin Modern Poets vol. 11*	Penguin
Adrienne Rich	*Poems: Selected and New 1950–74*	Norton

Anne Ridler	*New and Selected Poems*	Faber
Theodore Roethke	*Selected Poems*	Faber
Michael Rosen	*You Tell Me* (with Roger McGough)	Puffin
Colin Rowbotham	*Total Recall*	Littlewood Press
Irina Ratushinskaya	*Pencil Letter*	Bloodaxe
Vernon Scannell	*New and Collected Poems 1950–80*	Robson Books
Jon Silkin	*Selected Poems*	Routledge
Stevie Smith	*Two in One*	Longman
Marin Sorescu	*Selected Poems*	Bloodaxe
	The Biggest Egg in the World	
Wole Soyinka	*Idanre and Other Poems*	Methuen
Anne Stevenson	*The Fiction Makers*	OUP
R. S. Thomas	*Selected Poems 1946–68*	Bloodaxe
Isobel Thrilling	*The Ultrasonics of Snow*	Rivelin Grapheme Press
Anthony Thwaite	*Inscriptions*	OUP
Clive Webster	*Poetry Without Palm Trees*	Writers' Club Associates

3 A selection of anthologies, listed alphabetically by editor

Fleur Adcock	*The Faber Book of Twentieth Century Women's Poetry*	Faber
Michael and Peter Benton	*Touchstones* volumes 1–5, revised edition	Hodder & Stoughton
James Berry	*News For Babylon*	Chatto & Windus
Jeni Couzyn	*Contemporary Women Poets: Eleven British Writers*	Bloodaxe
Joan Goody	*Caribbean Anthology*	ILEA Learning Materials Centre
Seamus Heaney and Ted Hughes	*The Rattle Bag*	Faber
Roger McGough	*Strictly Private*	Penguin
Jack Mapanje and Landeg White	*Oral Poetry from Africa*	Longman
Gerald Moore and Ulli Beier	*Modern African Poetry*	Penguin
D. Scott	*Bread and Roses*	Virago
Morag Styles	*I Like That Stuff*	Cambridge
Morag Styles	*You'll Love This Stuff*	Cambridge
Geoffrey Summerfield	*Worlds*	Penguin
Anthony Thwaite	*Six Centuries of Verse*	Methuen/Thames Television

GLOSSARY OF TECHNICAL TERMS

There are scores of technical terms to describe different poetic structures and techniques: fortunately, it is perfectly possible to talk intelligently and sensitively about poetry using very few of them. Nonetheless, we have found it helpful to use several of them once or twice at least in the course of this book and have listed those that appear in the text along with a few others that you are likely to come across and that you may yourself find it helpful to use as you gain more confidence in talking and writing about poetry.

alliteration   (note the spelling: NOT **ill. . !**)   When the same consonant sound is repeated in words or syllables in close succession. It usually refers to the repetition of a sound or letter at the beginning of words, as in

> He clasps the crag with hooked hands

where the repetition of the *c* and *h* helps the sound to echo the meaning when we say the line aloud, but it can appear elsewhere in the line as in:

> Fields ever fresh and groves ever green

where, apart from the repetition of *f* and *g* there is a less noticeable repetition of the letter *v*. In this book, 'Esther's Tomcat' on p. 56 offers many examples.

assonance   The echoing of similar vowel sounds in the same line or consecutive lines. Thus *place* and *fade* are assonance.

ballad   a narrative poem (i.e. one that tells a story) usually written in four line stanzas rhyming *abcb* or *abab*. It may have a repeated refrain (i.e. a line or verse that is repeated at certain fixed points in the poem). The language is usually simple.

blank verse   Verse composed of an indefinite number of unrhymed iambic pentameters. Most of Shakespeare's plays and much of Wordsworth's poetry are in blank verse. The passage on p. 97 is an example of blank verse from Wordsworth. (See **iambic pentameter** under **rhythm, stress, metre** below.)

consonant   A speech sound which is not a vowel, for example b, c, d, f, g, h, j are consonants. Consonants are combined with a vowel to make a syllable. (See **vowel**.)

couplet   A pair of lines usually of the same metre which have a common rhyme, as in

> True ease in writing comes from art, not chance,
> As those move easiest who have learned to dance.

free verse   Poetry which has no regular metre or rhyme pattern as, for example, 'Dissection' on p. 10. Properly, the content and mood of the poem suggest its form or shape on the page.

haiku   A form of tightly structured formal Japanese poem which properly has seventeen syllables arranged in three lines of five, seven and five syllables. This rule is often broken in translations of haiku into English where stress rather than syllable counting is more important.

image/imagery Images in poetry are pictures or sense impressions conveyed in words by the writer. An image in poetry is one which has a direct appeal to one or more of our five senses and will often involve a comparison between two or more usually unrelated objects (see **simile** and **metaphor**). One can talk about the images Ted Hughes uses in 'The Warm and the Cold' (p. 35) or about Ted Hughes's imagery.

irony/ironic Irony is when a writer suggests a meaning which might be quite different, even opposite to the one he or she *appears* to offer us. Sarcasm is a very simple form of irony intended to hurt the listener: for example when we say *O, very clever!* in a sneering tone we mean the opposite of what we have said. We may sometimes say something is ironic when the opposite of what we might have expected actually happens and causes a certain amount of amusement.

metaphor A direct comparison of one thing with another without the introductory *like* or *as*. Sylvia Plath's poem 'Metaphors' on p. 43 is a series of such direct comparisons. Describing her pregnancy she writes she is 'An elephant, a ponderous house/A melon strolling on two tendrils'; she does not write that she is *like* an elephant, etc. The poem 'Cock-Crow' on p. 25 also uses several metaphors e.g. 'the wood of thoughts' and 'sharp axe of light'. Such comparison is at the heart of poetry and like simile it yokes together in words, and so in the images in our minds, things we had not previously connected. Louis Untermeyer wrote: 'Its element is surprise. To relate the hitherto unrelated, to make the strange seem familiar and the familiar seem strange is the aim of metaphor. Through this heightened awareness, poetry, though variously defined, is invariably pronounced and unmistakably perceived.'

mood or **tone** The prevailing state of mind or feeling of the poem which the writer appears to suggest to the reader and the overall emotional effect it generates. For example, one might speak of the sombre or lively tone or mood of the poem.

onomatopoeia A word whose sound imitates and therefore suggests its meaning as in bow-wow, hiss, whizz, crackle, cuckoo.

parody A piece of writing which imitates the characteristics of a writer's style with the intention of making fun of it.

pastiche A piece of writing which imitates the characteristics of a writer's style.

personification Giving human shape or characteristics to something non-human e.g. an animal or an inanimate object as in Sylvia Plath's poem 'Mirror' on p. 48; or addressing an inanimate object or abstract quality as though it were a person as in

> O Moon, look down from thy silver sphere

quatrain A four line stanza or group of lines which may have various rhyme schemes. The commonest verse form in English.

rhyme Identity of sound between words or verse lines in which the vowel and closing consonant sounds of a stressed syllable are repeated together with any weak syllables which may follow. In poetry, the letter or letters preceding the accented vowel must be *unlike* in sound e.g. *right* and *fight* which is a **perfect** or **complete rhyme** with two identically pronounced consonants (*t*) two identically pronounced vowels (*i*), a difference in the previous consonant (*r* and *f*), and two identical stress patterns. *Right* and *fight* are **one-syllable** or **single rhymes** but there are also **double** and **triple rhymes** as in the two or three syllable *making* and *baking* or *slenderly* and *tenderly*. One syllable rhymes are sometimes known as **masculine rhyme** and two syllable rhymes as **feminine rhyme**. Some rhymes may now appear incorrect simply because the pronunciation of words has changed over the years – *love/move, wind/mind* are common examples of what is sometimes known as **eye rhyme**. A writer may sometimes choose to soften the effect of rhyme by using **half rhyme** or **para rhyme** in which the consonant or the vowel is different. Wilfred Owen's poems 'Exposure' and 'Strange Meeting' make frequent use of this device, with half rhymes of words such as *brambles/rumbles, years/yours, spoiled/spilled*. Another common device is **internal rhyme** where a rhyme is used in the middle as well as at the end of a line as in:

> And pillows bright where tears may light

rhyme scheme   The conventional way of noting the pattern of rhymed line endings in a stanza or a group of lines. The letter *a* is used for the first rhymed sounds, *b* for the second and so on. Thus we can say that the rhyme scheme of both 'Mary, Mary Magdalene' (p. 41) and of 'The Tom Cat' (p. 55) is *abcb* (but watch out for the occasional internal rhymes in the former). The poem 'Cock-Crow' (p. 25) is arranged in couplets and its rhyme scheme is *aa, bb*, etc.

rhythm, stress, metre   Rhythms and metres in English poetry are based on stress – the emphasis which we give certain syllables in *spoken* English. The pattern of groups of stressed and unstressed syllables in poetry together make up its rhythm. Thus when we say *Monday* the first syllable *Mon* is stressed and the second *day* is weak, whereas when we say *amuse* this pattern is reversed. The classic approach is to suggest that we can indicate patterns if we mark the weak and strong stresses in a line by using / to indicate a strong stress and x to indicate a weak one. In the line

> x / x / x / x /   x   /
> A book of verses underneath the bough

we can see that there are ten syllables to the line which fall into five pairs, each with an unstressed syllable followed by a stressed one. This unstressed/stressed pair is very common in English verse and is known as an **iambic foot**. Where, as here, there are five such iambic feet in a line, it is called an **iambic pentameter** (*penta-* simply meaning *five* as, for example, in *pentagon*). Other lines containing different numbers of feet (from one to eight) are monometer (1), dimeter (2), trimeter (3), tetrameter (4), hexameter (6), heptameter (7) and octameter (8).

After the iambic foot, the trochaic foot (stressed followed by unstressed: /x) is probably the most common in English verse

> /   x   /   x   /   x / x
> Home art gone and ta'en thy wages

There are several other patterns of syllables that according to classic tradition make up other different feet in English poetry such as the dactylic foot (stressed followed by two unstressed: /x x) and the spondaic foot (two stressed syllables: //) but we suggest that if you wish to pursue the matter further you should look to a specialist book such as *How Poetry Works* by Philip Davies Roberts (Penguin, 1986). You will find that in practice, stress patterns in English poetry are subtle and varied and that rhythms are rarely banged out in the mechanical manner that is perhaps suggested by applying classical rules of Latin scansion. It is more helpful for you to be able to hear and enjoy the dancing rhythm in this line

> Love again, song again, nest again, young again

than to know that it could be said to consist of four dactylic feet.

run-on line(s)/enjambement   Run-on lines of verse occur where the structure and meaning carry the reader's eye and ear directly over to the next line without a break. Enjambement reinforces this effect by ensuring that the second line has a weak rather than a strong opening syllable so that any break is even less noticeable.

simile   (pronounced *simmily*: note the plural is **similes** pronounced *simmilies*)   A comparison between two things introduced by the words *like* or *as*. Ted Hughes's poem 'The Warm and the Cold' on p. 35 contains over a dozen such similes e.g. 'The badger in its bedding/Like a loaf in the oven. (See also the notes on **metaphor** and **imagery** above.)

sonnet   A poem of fourteen lines, each line being typically an iambic pentameter of ten syllables. The two main types are the **English** or **Shakespearean sonnet**, consisting of twelve lines made up of three quatrains (*abab, cdcd, efef*) plus a concluding couplet (*gg*) and the **Italian** or **Petrarchan** sonnet consisting of an octave and a concluding sestet. The octave is eight lines in two quatrains rhyming *abba, abba*: the sestet is composed of six lines rhyming *cdc, dcd*; or *cde, cde*; or *cd, cd, cd*. The **Miltonic** sonnet is based on the Petrarchan form but there is no pause between the octave and sestet – which generally rhymes *cd, cd, cd*.

stanza   Another word for a verse in poetry. A stanza has at least three lines, more often four and is usually rhymed in a pattern which is repeated throughout the poem.

stress   All English speech has set rhythms of stressed and weak syllables. There is an agreed way of saying *Eng-lish* with an emphasis – or stress – on the first syllable *Eng-*; similarly the word *syllable* has a stress on its own first syllable.

syllable   Words may be broken down into their constituent syllables – the small speech sounds that go to make them up. Thus *bro-ken* has two syllables; *down* has only one; *un-der-neath* has three . . . and so on. A syllable must include a central vowel and may be preceded by as many as three and followed by up to four consonant sounds. The way in which words are split into syllables in English is fairly arbitrary so don't worry too much about it: trust your ear rather than any mechanical principle. In a word with several syllables, one syllable receives the main stress though others may receive secondary stress and may be regarded as strong or weak according to what seems to suit the poem's metre.

syllabic verse   Verse in which the total number of syllables in each line is regular. The poem 'Metaphors' on p. 43 has nine syllables to each and every line. In practice, the number of stresses per line, not the number of syllables is what most English readers notice.

symbol   Something regarded by most people as naturally typifying, representing or recalling something else because it has similar qualities or because it is generally associated with it. Thus white is a symbol of purity, the cross is a symbol of Christianity, the lion is a symbol of courage.

vowel   An open and prolonged speech-sound made by using the mouth as a resonator as air is exhaled. A vowel can be a syllable on its own as *a* for example. The letters representing vowels are a, e, i, o, u.

LIST OF POEMS QUOTED IN THE TEXT

Anonymous	Shantytown
Fleur Adcock	The Telephone Call
Maya Angelou	Song for the Old Ones
William Blake	The Sick Rose
Valerie Bloom	Wha fe Call I'
Alan Brownjohn	Cat
Charles Causley	The Prodigal Son
	Mary, Mary Magdalene
Tony Connor	A Child Half-Asleep
U. A. Fanthorpe	Men on Allotments
	Dear Mr Lee
Robert Frost	The Lockless Door
	Nothing Gold Can Stay
Thomas Hardy	Men Who March Away
Tony Harrison	Fire-eater
A. L. Hendricks	Hot Summer Day
Phoebe Hesketh	Clown
	Solo
	Sally
	The Paint Box
Ted Hughes	The Warm and the Cold
	Esther's Tomcat
Kathleen Jamie	Jane
Arun Kolatkur	The Butterfly
Philip Larkin	Born Yesterday
Richard Lovelace	To Lucasta, Going Beyond the Seas
Norman MacCaig	Neighbour

— *Acknowledgments* —

The authors and publishers would like to thank the following for permission to reproduce material in this volume.

Press Poetry for 'A Child Half-Asleep' by Tony Connor from *New Selected Poems* (1982); The Associated Examining Board for AEB GCE A Level English Alternative Syllabus examination material; Basic Books Publishers for 'First Frost' by Andrei Voznesensky trans. Stanley Kunitz from P. Blake and M. Hayward (eds) *Antiworlds and The Fifth Ace: Poems by Andrei Voznesensky* (1966); Bloodaxe Books for 'Jane' by Kathleen Jamie from *The Way We Live* by Kathleen Jamie and for poems by Marin Sorescu from *The Biggest Egg in The World* by Marin Sorescu, translated by eight British and Irish poets including Joana Russell-Gebbett and David Constantine with Joana Russell-Gebbett (1987); Bogle L'Ouverture Publications Limited for 'Wha Fe Call I' by Valerie Bloom from *Touch Mi: Tell Me*; Century Hutchinson for 'Lady Godiva' by Irina Ratushinskaya from *Pencil Letter* by Irina Ratushinskaya; Doubleday for 'The Tom-Cat' by Don Marquis from *Poems and Portraits* by Don Marquis; Enitharmon Press for 'The Clown', 'Solo', 'Sally' and 'Paint Box' all by Phoebe Hesketh from *New and Collected Poems: Netting The Sun* by Phoebe Hesketh (1989); Faber and Faber Limited for 'The Warm and the Cold' by Ted Hughes from *Season Songs*, 'The Stag' by Ted Hughes and 'Esther's Tomcat' by Ted Hughes from *Lupercal*, 'In a Station of the Metro' by Ezra Pound from *Collected Shorter Poems*, 'Mare Nostrum' and 'At Parting' by Anne Ridler from *New Selected Poems*; The Estate of Robert Frost and Edward Connery Lathem and Henry Holt and Co. Inc. for 'The Lockless Door' and 'Nothing Gold Can Stay' by Robert Frost from Edward Connery Lathem (ed.) *The Poetry of Robert Frost* published by Jonathan Cape Limited; Tony Harrison for 'Fire-eater' from *Selected Poems* published by Penguin Books; A. L. Hendricks for 'Hot Summer Day'; Olwyn Hughes for 'Metaphors' and 'Mirror' by Sylvia Plath from *Collected Poems* by Sylvia Plath published by Faber and Faber Limited, copyright Ted Hughes 1967, 1971 and 1981; Arun Kolatkur for 'The Butterfly' from Morag Styles (ed.) *I Like That Stuff* published by Cambridge University Press; London and East Anglia Group for LEAG GCSE examination material; Leslie Norris for 'July the Seventh'; Norman MacCaig for 'Neighbour' from *Voice Over* published by Chatto and Windus; Macmillan, London and Basingstoke for 'Cat' by Alan Brownjohn from *Brownjohn's Beasts* (1970) and for 'The Prodigal Son' and 'Mary, Mary Magdalene' by

Charles Causley from *Collected Poems*; The Marvell Press for 'Born Yesterday' by Philip Larkin, first published in *The Less Received*; Mautolglade Music for 'Richard Cory' by Paul Simon (1966); New Directions for 'A Negro Woman' by William Carlos Williams from *Pictures from Breughel*; Oxford University Press for 'Telephone Call' by Fleur Adcock reprinted from *The Incident Book* by Fleur Adcock (1986); Peterloo Poets for 'Men on Allotments' by U. A. Fanthorpe from *Side Effects* (1978) and *Selected Poems* published by Peterloo Poets and King Penguin (1986) and for 'Dear Mr Lee' by U. A. Fanthorpe from *A Watching Brief* (1987); Random House for 'Song for the Old Ones' by Maya Angelou; Robson Books for 'Growing Pain' by Vernon Scannell from *New and Collected Poems* by Vernon Scannell; Routledge for 'First Ice' (illustration) by Kristina Nutall from *Young Readers Responding to Poems* by M. Benton, J. Tesey, R. Bell and K. Hurst (1988); Colin Rowbotham for 'Dissection' and 'Moonfall', the latter from *Total Recall* published by Littlewood Press; Stanley Thorne for 'Manwatching' by Georgina Garrett from *I See A Voice* by Michael Rosen Hutchinson (1982); Transworld Publishers for 'First Ice' by Andrei Voznesensky trans. George Reavey from Barnstone and Willes (eds) *Modern European Poets*, Bantam Books (1966); Virago Press for 'The Fat Black Woman Goes Shopping' by Grace Nichols, copyright Grace Nichols (1984); Clive Webster for 'Fe Tek A Stride'; The Welsh Joint Education Committee for WJECZ GCSE English Literature examination material; 'Richard Cory' from *The Children of the Night* by Edwin Arlington Robinson courtesy of Scribner's New York (1897).

Special thanks and acknowledgment are also due to the following:

Colin Rowbotham for supplying drafts of 'Moonfall' and allowing us to reprint them; Phoebe Hesketh for supplying drafts of 'Paint Box' and for allowing us to print them; John Teasey, Head of English at Robert Mays' School, Odiham, Hants, for allowing us to reproduce several examples of his pupils' work, notably that of Sara, Elizabeth and Kristina; and for permission to reproduce his sheet on the poetry journal (sections 4 and 10); Ros Sutton, Swanmore School, Southampton, for Marian's work in section 9; Alec Roberts, formerly Head of English at The Bohunt School, Liphook, Hants for Steven's work in section 10; Clive Webster for his poem 'Fe Tek A Stride' and for kindly supplying the additional notes.